HISTORY OF THE MALAY KINGDOM OF PATANI

SEJARAH KERAJAAN MELAYU PATANI

T0307862

CONNER BAILEY received the B.A. in History from Southern Oregon College in 1968 and subsequently spent three years in the Peace Corps, working in a rural health clinic just south of the Malaysia-Thailand border. In 1974 he received the Master of International Studies degree from Ohio University, and in 1980 he received the Ph.D. in Rural Sociology from Cornell University. Between 1980 and 1982, he was a Senior Research Fellow with the International Center for Living Aquatic Resources Management (ICLARM), engaged in field work in the Philippines and Indonesia. Subsequently, he was a Research Fellow in the Marine Policy and Ocean Management Center, Woods Hole Oceanographic Institution. Currently he is a professor in the Department of Agriculture, Economics, and Rural Sociology at Auburn University, Auburn, Alabama 36849.

JOHN N. MIKSIC received the B.A. in Anthropology from Dartmouth College in 1968. In the Peace Corps, he served in the Department of Agriculture (Kedah) and later as a teacher (Penang) in Malaysia. He received the Master of International Studies degree from Ohio University in 1974 and the Ph.D. in Anthropology from Cornell University in 1979. Between 1979 and 1981, he was a regional planning advisor in Bengkulu, Indonesia. Subsequently he was a Project Specialist in Archaeology with the Asian Cultural Council and a lecturer in Archaeology at Universitas Gadjah Mada, Yogyakarta, and at Universitas Indonesia, Jakarta. At present he teaches archaeology at the National University of Singapore, Kent Ridge, Singapore 0511.

HISTORY OF THE MALAY KINGDOM OF PATANI

SEJARAH KERAJAAN MELAYU PATANI

by

Ibrahim Syukri
(pseudonym)

Translated by

Conner Bailey and John N. Miksic

Ohio University Center for International Studies
Monographs in International Studies

Southeast Asia Series Number 68
Athens, Ohio 1985

Library of Congress Cataloging in Publication Date

Ibrahim Syukri.
  History of the Malay Kingdom of Patani.

  (Monographs in international studies. Southeast Asia series no. 68)
  Translation of: Sejarah Kerajaan Melayu Patani.
  Bibliography: p.
  1. Patani (Kingdom)--History.   2. Malays (Asian people)--
Thailand--History. I. Title. II. Series. DS588.P29I2713   1984
959.5'1   84-18967   ISBN 0-89680-123-3

Reprinted 1990

ISBN 0-89680-123-3

CONTENTS

MAPS

vi

FOREWORD

It is not unusual for academics to consider themselves the sole legitimate guardians and custodians of history, dismissing as antiquarians or amateurs, in the most pejorative sense of the word, writers of local and regional history who lack scholarly credentials. It is customary, for example, to take seriously such early "traditional" works as the *Sejarah Melayu* or the Luang Prasoet version of the Chronicles of Ayudhya, but to dismiss as beneath contempt the work of non-professional Southeast Asian historians in the twentieth century. The contemporary reader is left with two distinct bodies of materials through which to study Southeast Asian history in Western languages: the all-too-few translations of the classical, pre-modern indigenous annals and chronicles; and a growing body of scholarly works covering both pre-modern and modern times, replete with footnotes and all the usual scholarly apparatus. Together, these sources threaten to engulf the few indigenous "traditional" voices that have persisted.

This process attests to a seemingly inexorable signification of "history" in Western terms, to denote historians commitment to the idea–explicitly or implicitly–that there exists a real, knowable, objective past that can be uncovered by systematic and rational means, as if each footnote were a nail to fix in place the "facts" that, taken together, constitute The Past. Almost completely neglected, most especially by academics, is another kind of history and–dare we admit it?–an even larger group of historians that both now and in the long run have far greater influence upon the historical consciousness of those who live it, those whose history it is: the "amateur" local and regional historians within Southeast Asia who, relatively unexposed to Western scholarly styles and canons, and free from the obligation to be somehow "objective," write about their own history from the inside, expressing unselfconsciously their own values, local perspectives, and, not least, political hopes and aspirations.

It is not as easy to identify these indigenous writers as it might at first appear. They are not simply anachronistic perpetuators of "traditional" historiography, for it is difficult to imagine that any such creatures ever existed, blindly handing on the memories of one generation to another. Even Southeast Asian annalists of the sixteenth through eighteenth centuries partook of the fruits of learning of their day, and Malay annalists probably knew as much of Islamic and western Asian historiography as the sixteenth-century chroniclers of Chiang Mai knew of Buddhist, Singhalese historiography. Similarly, local historians in mid-twentieth century Southeast Asia often display knowledge both of the "national" history taught in their schools and of at least fragments of Western scholarship and writing bearing on the history of their region. Here the best examples probably include those authors who write of the Srivijaya period in the history of the Malay Peninsula, or of the era of Majapahit imperialism, whose works in both instances owe much to the accumulated results of Western-style scholarship on their subjects, but also usually go far beyond what Western historians would consider the best evidence would allow.

One might hypothesize that local historical traditions and activities flourish in inverse relation to the strength of central, national government control or, better, that local historiography is most likely to flourish either when it does not matter at all (that is, does not challenge the existing political structure, as in contemporary Chiang Mai where there has recently been a great revival of local historiography), or when it matters a great deal, as in the case of the book we have here.

Over more than a millennium the Malay kingdom of Patani survived, its last ruler dying within living memory. This existence, however, often was tenuous: the kingdom was secure only when its most distant neighbors were weak or distracted, and it was perennially their prey when their power or circumstances permitted. Leaving aside ancient Langkasuka, a kingdom about which little is known other than it probably was located from the

viii

sixth- to thirteenth-centuries in the valley of the Patani River (Wheatley 1961:252-65). Patani grew to its greatest power in the sixteenth and seventeenth centuries in the wake of the fall of the sultanate of Malacca to the Portuguese in 1511, only subsequently to decline amidst the general disarray of the Malay and maritime world that accompanied Western intrusions and Chinese trade in the late seventeenth and eighteenth centuries. In the nineteenth century Patani fell within the orbit of Siamese and British expansion, ultimately becoming caught between Siam and Britain and, by the Anglo-Siamese Treaty of 1909, remaining in Siam when its Malay neighbors to the south and west were ceded to British Malaya. In the eighty years since, Patani increasingly, if reluctantly, has been drawn into the Thai nation-state, a process that has not been without conflict or resistance which continues to the present day.

At various points in this long history, the people of Patani have felt impelled to recall and make known its history. The *Hikayat Patani*, a composite text dating apparently from the early eighteen century, is the first and best-known of their efforts.[1] The *Sejarah Kerajaan Melayu Patani* (History of the Malay Kingdom of Patani) that we have here, though separated from the first by some two centuries, is just as important in its own way, for it gives voice to the pained historical consciousness of Patani in the late 1940s and early 1950s, when the full force of Thailand's policies of national integration began to bear upon the Malays of the Peninsula.

We know little of the book and its author. It clearly was written under the force of the passions unleashed as postwar Thai governments began aggressively to apply to the Malays the policies for cultural, linguistic, educational, and legal assimilation designed perhaps initially to compel the assimilation of Thailand's large Chinese minority (see Haemindra 1976, 1977; Koch 1977). The violence that accompanied these efforts brought Patani into the international spotlight in 1948 before world attention shifted to major nationalist and communist insurrection elsewhere. Above all else, perhaps, this book might be regarded as an expression of that crisis, both as an immediate political situation and as a long-term reflection of the context out of which it exploded.

The author of this *Sejarah* pseudonymously identifies himself as "Ibrahim Syukri," about whom nothing else is known. We can tell from his book that he clearly was a native of Patani well-educated in his local traditions and culture (to the point of writing in the Arabic-derived *jawi* script). It also is apparent that the author had obtained a degree of Western-style learning, even including some knowledge of English (which he would have had great difficulty in obtaining in the Patani region). He published this book not in Patani but in Pasir Putih, across the frontier in Kelantan. Because its political stance challenged both Thai rule and Thai-Malaysian relations, the book was suppressed in both countries, and few copies appear to have survived.

Because the *Sejarah* was published in Malay using the jawi script, it is clear that its author intended it only for a local audience. Jawi is in wide use in Thailand's southern border provinces; it also is used widely in Malaysia, though as a primary medium jawi in that country has given way to romanized Malay (*rumi*). We can reasonably conclude that the author was not attempting to mobilize a wider Malay (or Indonesian) opinion, for which he would have employed the Roman script; nor did he express himself in Thai or English, both of which languages he apparently knew. He was addressing a local audience, within an intimate context of shared values, and for political purposes, in order to persuade, mobilize, and inform his fellows.

It would be unfair to judge "Ibrahim Syukri" as an historian on the basis of this book, though he would by no means earn dismissal from dispassionately "objective" professionals: among other things, he brings forward much material not available elsewhere (see Volume I of Teeuw and Wyatt 1970:46-49). It is more useful, and ultimately more rewarding, to take the *Sejarah Kerajaan Melayu Patani* as a "text," no less and no more, like the *Sejarah Melayu* or the *Hikayat Patani*. As such, it has much to teach us about the history of the Malay community of south Thailand. But, having said that, do we not fall again into the trap with which we began, the sterile intellectual prison of objective, rational "facts" and "history"? Perhaps an encounter with "Ibrahim Syukri" should bring us to hesitate to reduce *him* to *our* purposes, and lead us instead to an appreciation of *his*. He deserves to be taken at least as seriously as the early Malay annalists or Chiang Mai chroniclers.

David K. Wyatt
Cornell University
Ithaca, New York

TRANSLATORS' INTRODUCTION

The Historical Setting

The Malay Peninsula projects south for a thousand miles from the mainland mass of Southeast Asia and divides the waters of the Indian Ocean from those of the South China Sea. The Kra Isthmus is approximately in the middle of this peninsula, which here narrows to fifty miles. The Patani region lies on the east coast of the peninsula, just south of the Kra Isthmus. This narrow waist of the peninsula has for centuries been a zone of contact between different peoples, including the Austronesians, the Mon-Khmer, and the Thai inhabitants of Southeast Asia, as well as foreign travelers from further north, east, and west whose routes frequently intersected here (Teeuw and Wyatt 1970:7; Wales 1974; Wheatley 1961).

Chinese envoys visited this region in the second century A.D. in order to gather information on commercial activity. Numerous archaeological remains of long-distance trade found in the area date from at least as early as the eighth century A.D. These include such artifacts as an inscription in Tamil and associated south Indian religious statuary, and numerous remains of trade goods including Middle Eastern glass, and pottery of both Persian and Chinese provenance (Lamb 1961; O'Connor 1972).

Various descriptions of the region compiled by Chinese and Arab writers during the first millennium A.D. give the impression that the peninsula during that period was divided among a number of small principalities. These polities seem to have maintained a considerable degree of internal autonomy while acknowledging the general suzerainty of more powerful kingdoms to the north and south whose interest in the isthmian region was excited primarily by its strategic location on maritime trade routes. It is probable that the rare and precious but light-weight items involved in long-distance trade between the peoples of the Indian Ocean and the South China Sea were brought by ship to the isthmus, unloaded there and portaged to the opposite shore. This strategy was particularly popular when the narrow Straits of Malacca were subject to outbreaks of piracy. During the late ninth century, when the Tang dynasty was in its death throes and foreign merchants fled from the massacres which took place in the Chinese ports open to them, the area near Chaiya formed an important rendezvous for Chinese and Arab merchants. To a somewhat lesser extent, foreign interest in the region was stimulated by such local products as tree resins, gold, and tin.

The Malay empire of Sriwijaya probably held sway over the southern half of the peninsula, including the Kra region, by the late seventh century A.D., but had lost it by the beginning of the eleventh century (Briggs 1951:286; Wolters 1958). At the same time Khmer influences enter the art and epigraphy of the region. The indigenous stratum lying beneath these external influences, however, is still almost completely unknown (O'Connor 1975).

In the late thirteenth century the Chinese imperial court was aware of hostilities in the northern peninsula between the *Ma-li-yu-erh* and the *T'ai*, who were extending their domains south from their capital of Sukothai (Wheatley 1961:301), in the process incorporating many small principalities which formerly had been Khmer dependencies. Siamese naval expeditions during the fourteenth and fifteenth centuries sailed as far south as Singapore. During the first half of the seventeenth century the kingdom of Siam launched four unsuccessful invasions of Patani before finally defeating this Malay kingdom in 1784. Patani's Malay population revolted in defiance of Siameze suzerainty in 1791, 1808, and 1831, but each time were suppressed militarily. During the nineteenth and twentieth centuries Patani's local autonomy gradually was eroded as this once independent kingdom was broken up and absorbed by the kingdom of Siam.

In 1909 the British negotiated a settlement with Siam which recognized the latter's claim over Patani in return for Siamese acknowledgement that Kedah and Kelantan, as well as the other Malay states to the south, fell within the British sphere of influence. This Anglo-Siamese treaty established the border which separates present-day Thailand from Malaysia and led to the isolation of Patani's Malay Muslims from their brethren to the south. Today the population of Patani, Yala, and Narathiwat provinces–the core of the old Patani kingdom–is still largely Malay and Muslim and constitutes a national minority restive under what many of them perceive to be cultural, political, and economic domination by the Thai Buddhist majority. The long history of tension and sometimes violent conflict between these two proud peoples continues to bear unhappy consequences to this day.

The Sejarah Kerajaan Melayu Patani

Indigenous sources for the study of isthmian history are limited to "oral legends and written chronicles, some of very considerable antiquity" which, however, with "their blending of myth, literature, and history demand of those who would use them high critical skills" (Wyatt 1975:3).

The *Sejarah Kerajaan Melayu Patani* (History of the Malay Kingdom of Patani)–SKMP–presents a distinctly Malay interpretation of Patani's history. The SKMP is of interest to scholars interested in this region primarily as it is one of the rare works to address from a Malay perspective the problems of contemporary southern Thailand and their historical antecedents. As such, Professor Wyatt's cautionary comments regarding the accuracy of local histories such as the SKMP, quoted above, are apt. So too, however, are the observations by Wyatt presented in the Foreword to this volume, where he argues that manuscripts such as the SKMP are important documents in their own right and on their own terms, particularly as they play an important role in maintaining historical consciousness among the people most intimately concerned.

The author of the SKMP ambitiously has attempted to survey the history of the region from the arrival of its first human inhabitants to the late 1940s, when the undated manuscript was published privately in Pasir Putih, Kelantan, under the pseudonym "Ibrahim Syukri." The author, who is ethnically Malay and both a citizen and a civil servant of Thailand, is otherwise unknown to the translators, who obtained a photocopy of his manuscript from the John M. Echols collection at Cornell University.

The SKMP was printed in jawi, Malay written in a slightly modified Arabic script. Among the Malay population of southern Thailand literacy in jawi is higher than that for romanized Malay. The book was not written for Western academics or other foreign readers but rather for the Malay population of Thailand's southern provinces. As such, the SKMP belongs to traditional isthmian rather than contemporary western historiography.

The author appears to have taken much of his information regarding Patani's early history from the *Hikayat Patani*, of which several slightly different manuscripts are known to exist. The *Hikayat Patani* itself is comprised of six parts, each probably written by different authors at different times during the late seventeenth and early eighteenth centuries. The *Hikayat Patani* has been the subject of an intensive linguistic and historical study by Teeuw and Wyatt (1970), who note that "There are . . . apart from the cases where Syukri refers explicitly to a Malay source, many pages in his book which are so close to our text that it is probable that Syukri must have had this particular hikayat at his disposal" (1970:47). However, in carrying his narrative beyond the eighteenth century, Syukri also draws on a number of other sources, including Western ones, employing them where needed to reinforce his basic arguments.

The SKMP is divided into four chapters, the first three of which are clearly within the Malay hikayat tradition. After tracing the origins of the area's first inhabitants (Chapter 1), the author describes the founding of Patani, the coming of Islam, and the growth of Patani as a major port of call for Siamese, Japanese, Portuguese, Dutch, and English traders during the sixteenth and seventeenth centuries (Chapter 2). In this second chapter, Patani is shown at the pinnacle of her prestige and power, repelling four Siamese invasions and participating in the sack of Ayuthia by Burmese forces. In Chapter 3, the author describes Patani's gradual decline during the eighteen century, her defeat and subjugation by Siam in 1784, the series of unsuccessful revolts which followed over the next fifty years, and the gradual dismantling of the kingdom as Patani's local autonomy gave way to direct rule from Bangkok.

In Chapter 4 the author moves from hikayat to polemic, issuing a strongly worded attack on twentieth century policies of the national government. The author traces the growth of organized Malay opposition from civil disobedience to open conflict between the Malays and the national government, which he characterizes as culturally and politically repressive and economically exploitative. He calls upon the Malays of southern Thailand to unite in shaping their own destiny but stops short of urging armed insurrection or recommending a specific political solution to the conflict which continues to plague this area over thirty years after the SKMP was written.

Syukri's presentation is at times unabashedly biased, but this is not exceptional within the Malay hikayat tradition. The SKMP places the conflict between Malay and Thai in an historical perspective and casts the Thais as villains of the plot. Syukri devotes considerable space to the description of historical Patani as a kingdom of wealth and fame. His aim is two-fold: to instill ethnic pride in the Malays of southern Thailand; and to contrast the conditions of a remembered "golden age" with those of today under the rule of the Thai government. Obviously, in evaluating the historical value of the text the reader must keep these aims of the author in mind.

The SKMP is not without interest for historians, however. Syukri has demonstrated that much of the material in the *Hikayat Patani* still has relevance for the Malays of southern Thailand. Among his accounts of the comings and goings of the rajas, sultans, and sultanas, Syukri has interspersed anecdotes which indicate that historical events and sites continue to be vital to the ethnic identity of the contemporary Malay population of Patani. His numerous references to archaeological sites in Patani also may be of value to future research in this field.

While Syukri refrained from advocating rebellion, his strongly-worded attack on the national government led to the banning of the SKMP in Thailand. Malaysia also banned the SKMP as a courtesy to a friendly neighboring country, and also perhaps to avoid any implication of official support for Malay irredentist or separatist causes.

Publication of this translation is not designed to exacerbate tensions in the region but rather to illuminate the dimensions of Malay ethnic consciousness and perceptions of the past in southern Thailand. It is the opinion of the translators that more is to be gained by including rather than excluding materials portraying the Malay viewpoint among the sources available for study of the continuing conflict in southern Thailand.

Notes on the Translation

As is commonly the case with translations, some balance must be struck between presenting the flavor and tone of the original manuscript and the need to make the text understandable to a foreign audience. Wherever possible, the translators have tried to follow the author's style. Often this proved difficult, however, as frequently we encountered whole paragraphs unmarked by any punctuation. Lewis (1954) notes that the absence of punctuation is common in jawi manuscripts. We have found it necessary in such cases to introduce punctuation marks to create coherent English sentences.

At a more conceptual level, we decided that certain key Malay terms could not to our satisfaction be translated into English with any degree of elegance. Readers with a modest familiarity with the Malay language should have no difficulty recognizing most of these terms (*raja muda, Siam-Asli*). To others our apologies and assurances that we have retained the original Malay only in a few cases and only where we deemed it most appropriate. Explanatory notes are provided.

Footnotes appearing at the bottom of the text are those of the author and are marked by single or double asterisks; translator's notes are numbered consecutively and located at the end of the manuscript.

The translators wish to acknowledge the assistance of and to dedicate this translation to the late Professor Emeritus John M. Echols. We began work on the SKMP while students of Professor

Echols, who in no way is responsible for any errors contained herein but who provided the stimulation without which this small contribution would not have appeared. We also wish to thank David Wyatt both for writing the Foreword and for his active encouragement as we worked on this manuscript.

Final preparation of this manuscript was supported in part by a grant from the Pew Memorial Trust to the Marine Policy and Ocean Management Center, Woods Hole Oceanographic Institution.

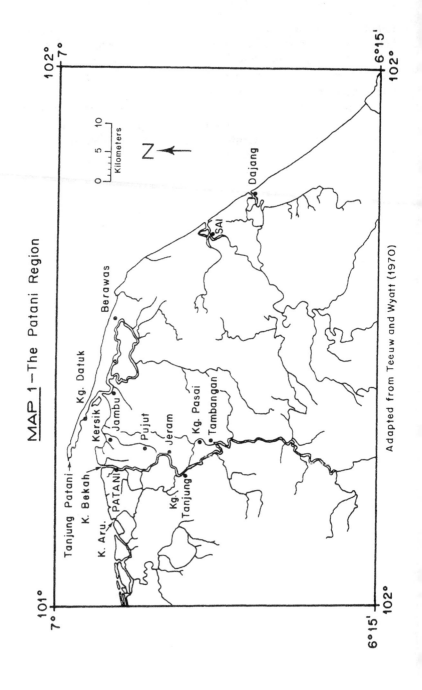

MAP 1—The Patani Region

Adapted from Teeuw and Wyatt (1970)

MAP 2

Geographic Divisions Within Patani During The Late Nineteenth Century

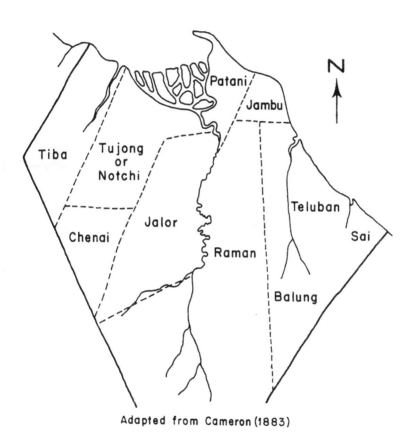

Adapted from Cameron (1883)

AUTHOR'S INTRODUCTION

Organizing and arranging this *Sejarah Kerajaan Melayu Patani* [History of the Malay Kingdom of Patani] was a very difficult task that consumed much time in order to achieve clarity and to ascertain the truth of actual events. During this time there were some old people in Patani who had written a few stories, but many of them were legends which were illogical or useless tales and not important to a precise history. They [the old people] were very secretive and the handwritten manuscripts were closely guarded and not mentioned to anyone. However, the writer struggled with great difficulty to gather these stories and to borrow or pay their owners for their use. Among these the writer received a hand-written manuscript which was particularly accurate and could be used as a guide in compiling this book.[2] To the owner of that manuscript this writer expresses a thousand thanks. Then the writer began personally to investigate old remains or traces that still are scattered around Patani to this day. The writer expended great effort and much time seeking additional information in history books written in foreign languages and in searching libraries so that finally the writer could put in order all the essentials so that this small book could come to exist.

The author believes that the arrangement and contents of this book do not include all events and changes which have occurred in the hundreds of years since the foundation of the Malay kingdom of Patani. The writer is especially concerned that there might be errors in this narrative or opinions written in this book, but the writer has proceeded because to this day there are no chronicles or histories written in the Malay language concerning the historical development of the Malay kingdom of Patani. To this day many Patani Malays are not aware of the circumstances concerning their kingdom in ancient times, that is, during the time

1

that the Malay kingdom of Patani was sovereign and in complete authority. It is to be hoped that with this small book they will be able to learn a little of the life and circumstances of their ancestors. It is especially hoped that this book will become something permanent for succeeding generations and will inspire them to study and compile more detailed books such as this.

Should the reader note mistakes in the writer's compilation, the writer greatly begs for pardon and constructive criticism in order to make corrections, and the writer expresses many thanks and best wishes.

Apologies and salutations from the author

Ibrahim Syukri

Chapter 1

MALAYA IN ANCIENT TIMES

Tanah Melayu

Malaya is a peninsula which stretches southward from and is situated at the southeastern part of the continent of Asia, possessing an extensive area.[3] Beginning in the north it stretches from the Kra Isthmus to the top of Malaya, including Singapura to the south.

In the north this peninsula joins Siam which is located between two kingdoms, on its left the kingdom of Burma and on its right the kingdom of Annam which is called French Indochina. The kingdoms of Siam, Annam, and Burma are located in a large peninsula, the peninsula of Indochina.

The peninsula of Malaya has two parts, the northern part and the southern. Its northern part begins at the Kra Isthmus and reaches to the provinces (*jajahan*) of Setul, Singgora, Yala, and Bengenera.[4] Currently the people of these provinces are included among the subjects of the kingdoms of Siam or Thailand. A large number of the inhabitants of the northern part of this peninsula are Siam-Thai, but in the six provinces of Setul, Cenak, Tiba, Patani, Yala, and Bengenera the majority are Malays.[5]

The southern part of this peninsula begins at the border of the Siam-Thai provinces previously mentioned down to the tip of the Malay peninsula, including the island of Singapura. In this part exist several Malay kingdoms today: Kedah, Perlis, Kelantan, Trengganu, Perak, Pahang, Selangor, Negeri Sembilan, Johor, Melaka, Pulau Pinang, and Singapura.

Although this peninsula has been called Malaya, the Malays were not the original people (*bangsa*) to inhabit it.[6] The Malays

3

were the last people to settle and reside in the peninsula after it had first been inhabited by several other peoples.

The first people to inhabit the peninsula of Malaya, according to information in history books, were people of a primitive type. Later it was settled by Hindus who came from India, after which it was ruled by the Siam-Asli who came from Siam.[7] Only later did the Malays arrive.

Briefly below there follows a short historical explanation of events in Malaya during ancient times.

There was a time a few hundred years before the birth of Christ when Malaya was not yet inhabited by civilized types of people as it is today. The land was covered with jungle and undergrowth and was inhabited by many kinds of wild animals.

Under the shelter of thick jungle and together with the wild animals there were two kinds of human beings of a primitive type who were able to make their own dwellings. They were the Semang (Pangan) people and the Sakai people.[8] Although both people are called human, actually their condition and way of life were still primitive, and far from the ways of civilized humans.

Several hundred years before the birth of Christ, the Hindus from India began to arrive in Malaya. At that time the Hindus had attained a high level of progress and culture in India. They arrived in Malaya with the intention of expanding their livelihood beyond their country. Malaya attracted them to come to this area of eastern Asia by its wealth, prosperity, and fame.

The path taken by the Hindus to East Asia at that time followed two routes, land and sea. By the land route they traveled via Burma, entering the lands of Siam and Annam. By the sea route they journeyed from India, sailing ships across the Indian Ocean, and entered Malaya and all the southern islands, including Sumatera, Java, Bali, Brunei, and others. They went as far as Siam, Cambodia, and Annam.

As a people which had a high culture in India, the Hindus possessed their own customs, traditions, and religion. Wherever they lived they firmly clung to their customs, traditions, and religion and they practiced them as though they were in their homeland of India.

Because the Hindus possessed a high culture with well-organized customs and traditions, the eastern inhabitants were

4

drawn to imitate or follow the actions of the Hindus. Eventually the Hindus became teachers who taught the inhabitants of the East their customs, traditions, and religion. In this way, as time passed, all inhabitants of the East completely accepted the customs and traditions of the Hindus.

Although the religion of the Hindus was of many kinds, nevertheless the best known were two religions, Brahmanism and Buddhism. Brahmanism is a religion that worships gods or goddesses and also ghosts and spirits and is divided into several sects according to which of the six gods are worshipped. Those who worship Siwa, for example, are therefore called people of the Siwa sect, while those who worship the god Vishnu are called people of the Vishnu sect and so on for the other sects.

The gods worshipped by the Hindus are very numerous and it would be of no use for us to mention them here. It is only necessary to note that this religion is the oldest in India and is still actively practiced. Meanwhile, more than two thousand years ago, there appeared a great teacher in India who purified the faith of India and taught a new faith called Buddhism to his followers.

When the great teacher Buddha died, Buddhism split into several sects, but among them were two major sects, Hinayana and Mahayana. The followers of the Hinayana sect, meaning "lesser vehicle," clung only to the teachings of the great teacher without alterations. At that time most of the followers of this sect were people of South India and therefore this sect came to be called *daksina nikaya*, meaning southern sect. In time the teaching of this sect withered away in India until finally it disappeared, except in Ceylon where it still is strong. In addition to the Indian followers of that sect, the Ceylonese, the present-day Siam-Thai remain faithful to this sect.

There is also the Mahayana sect, meaning "greater vehicle." The teachings of this sect have been much changed and altered according to the ideas of its followers. Some have added Brahmanic teachings so that there came into being far-reaching differences between the two sects, Hinayana and Mahayana. At that time the Mahayana sect was followed by the people of north India. Therefore this sect was called *utara nikaya* meaning northern sect, and its followers were called *maha nikaya*, people of

5

the Mahayana sect. The teachings of this sect through time became widespread and it is still strong in India. In the past this sect was most popular among people of the East, including those of Sumatera, Java, Bali, as well as the peninsula of Malaya. During the Time of Ignorance this sect was still strongly adhered to and believed in, as it is now by people in Annam, Cambodia, China, Japan, and Korea.[9]

The wide distribution of the Mahayana sect of the Buddhist religion to the East was brought about by people who came from India and spread their religion. The majority of them were from northern India, for example the country [negeri] of Kashmir and others.[10] Most numerous were Buddhists of the Mahayana sect.

Because of this, besides the followers of the Brahman religion there were also many people of the East who followed the Buddhist religion of the Mahayana sect. Only the Siam-Thai people firmly followed the Hinayana sect. When the Hindus arrived in the East they usually lived in groups. After they had grouped together, many of those places became countries. Malaya and other places then began to be developed. Hindus from India occasionally liked to act like rajas. When they began to settle in Malaya the desire to act like rajas did not disappear. When these countries were first established, Hindus began to be appointed as headmen or rajas to rule for the peace and safety of their people. Therefore each country had a raja governing it so that one after another countries were developed according to where there were Hindus gathered. At that time in the northern part of Malaya several countries were established, namely Tambralinga,[11] Gerahi,[12] Takkola,[13] Langkasuka (Kedah),[14] and others. All of these countries were ruled by Hindus. Tambralinggam is Nakhon Sri Thammarat or Ligor which now is ruled by Thailand.

The Hindus are a people who do not forget their customs, traditions, or religion. No matter where they reside they always practice them. When they began to attain power in Malaya they also built religious sanctuaries and other places of worship so that any place where Hindus have lived can be recognized from the remains and traces of such structures.

When the Hindus stayed in any place they always behaved well and mingled with the local residents. Finally they intermarried with them. Their descendants increased and because of this intermingling their descendants inherited authority over all regions of the East.

Here let us examine some matters regarding the inhabitants of the main peninsula of Indochina, the place which today constitutes the country of Siam, so that we may easily comprehend when matters concerning the Malays are mentioned.

In the time before the coming of the Hindus to the East the center of the Indochinese peninsula was inhabited by several peoples who possessed their own negeri and kingdoms. Whenever Hindus arrived, there occurred a situation similar to their arrival in Malaya, that is the Hindus were elevated by the local inhabitants to be their teachers. Thus it was not difficult for their religion to spread very easily and freely until finally almost all inhabitants in those countries had adopted the religions brought by the Hindus. The natives greatly respected and honored the Hindus until eventually there were those among them who desired to surrender sovereignty of their country to the Hindus, becoming like their servants.

In the center of the Indochinese peninsula at that time there existed three separate kingdoms, the kingdom of the Khmer people located in the east, the Lao kingdom located in the center of the peninsula, which has become the location of the country of Siam today, and third the kingdom of the Mon or Talaing people. Although these three peoples possessed their own individual governments, their customs and religion were identical except that the Mon and Khmer peoples were more influenced by the Hindus so that even their rajas were Hindus.

The system of government in the Lao kingdom at that time involved division into four territories and each had its own capital. Among these four territories the most famous was the territory known as Siam, and its capital also was called Siam.* This was the largest of the territories.

When the Thai who lived in the south of the country of China came to subjugate that region or territory their country was

---

*This country is now the territory of Sukothai which is located north of the territory of Bangkok.

7

given the name of Siam, and because of this until today the Thai are well-known and recognized by the world by the name of Siam.

These three kingdoms firmly maintained their individual power until the ninth century A.D. Only then did their situation change. The power of the Lao kingdom declined and it was subjugated by the Khmer people. Finally, the power of the Khmer was overthrown by the Thai, so that by the twelfth century A.D. all the land of Siam which had been in the power of the Khmer was completely under the authority of the Thai. Since then all the authority of the Khmer in Siam has been eliminated, as had that of the Lao.

In fact, these three kingdoms continually formed relationships with all other countries and kingdoms in all the islands in the south. At that time people from Siam began gradually to move south and gain a foothold in order to expand their livelihood.

Because those people came from Siam, the people in Malaya called them Siamese in order not to confuse them with the present-day Thai. Thus we call them the Siam-Asli, which means the Siamese who originally settled in Siam before the arrival of the modern-day Siam-Thai.

The coming of the Siam-Asli to Malaya was gradual, group by group. According to information in history books they arrived in Malaya during the fourth and fifth centuries A.D. During this long period there came to be many who settled in Malaya, after which the Siam-Asli began to share the power of the Hindus through associating and intermarrying with them. This finally caused the blood of the Hindus to mingle with the blood of the Siam-Asli and brought them the ancient power of the Hindus. Eventually the result of this mingling caused the Hindu rajas to change and become of Siam-Asli blood. Finally, by degrees, the power of the Hindus in Malaya fell into the hands of the Siam-Asli.

After the Siam-Asli gained power in Malaya they pushed on and went far to the south and also developed several countries in southern Malaya such as the countries of Gelanggayu,[15] Gangga Nagara,[16] Pahang, and others. At that time the Siam-Asli held power throughout Malaya.

Thus, the power of the Siam-Asli in Malaya endured for several hundred years until in the eighth century A.D. their power began to weaken, because at that time a kingdom of Malays was established in the islands of Sumatera, the kingdom of Srivijaya. This kingdom came to subjugate the countries of the Siam-Asli and finally the whole of Malaya was subject to the Srivijaya kingdom. The power of the Siam-Asli was completely destroyed. Moreover, at that time, the power of the Siam-Asli in the land of Siam was seized by the Thai who came from the south of the country of China so that the power of the Siam-Asli in Malaya was lost.

The original settlements of the Thai were in the districts of Southern China, in the territories of Szechwan, Yunan and others. Because the settlements of the Thai in China constantly were oppressed, crushed, and attacked by the Chinese, who were more powerful, the Thai gradually were forced to flee group by group and wander south through the center of the Indochinese peninsula. Wherever they found peace and safety from the oppression of the Chinese, there they made their country. After some time many countries were developed by the Thai in the region to the north of the country of Siam.

Among them there came a company of Thai who fled and developed a country near the region of Siam where the Khmer were then in control. Then the Thai began to attack and press against the power of the Khmer people until finally all the land of Siam was subjugated by the Thai. The Khmer were forced to flee to the southeast where they were able to re-establish a kingdom in the country of Cambodia which has endured until now.

Thus all the land of Siam was subjugated by the Thai, who established a kingdom of their own. Their power has endured so that the name of the Thai kingdom is widely known today.

Now let us investigate matters and affairs which concern the descent of the Malays and the place from which they originally came to settle in the Malay peninsula. There were ancestors of the Malays located in the island of Perca or Sumatera at the time of the arrival of the Hindus in Malaya.[17] Some of them [the Hindus] sailed eastward and arrived in the islands to the south and east of Malaya. To the island of Sumatera came the Hindus who settled and mingled with the original inhabitants of that island so that several kingdoms were established by the descendants of the Hindus.

9

At that time the region along the eastern and northern shores of Sumatera already was settled by a people who were called Jakun.[18] This people was not one of the primitive types of people which were in that island because they were more civilized than the primitive peoples. They preferred to inhabit regions by the seaside, whereas the primitive peoples greatly feared to live on the seashore and preferred to make their settlements inland, far from the water.

Although the Jakun communities were not organized into countries, nevertheless there were permanent settlements with their own leaders and they were skilled at making a living by such methods as fishing and so forth. Thus they knew how to make and to use boats and had the boldness to sail their boats far into the open sea to seek their living.

When the Hindus came and mingled with the Jakun people, they eventually brought forth children and grandchildren, and a new people was created who called themselves "Malays," meaning people of Malaya.

In fact these Malays were more advanced and civilized than their original ancestors because they had inherited culture and progress from two sides, that is from the Jakun people and from the Hindu people. These Malays followed the religions of their ancestors, that is Buddhism of the Mahayana sect or "maha nikaya" and the Brahman religion.

As the settlements of the Malays increased day by day, they were forced to move and seek for places to live throughout the world and these Malays developed several countries in Sumatera. Some went forth from the shores of Sumatera and sailed through the islands and great lands in the northeast of the continent of Asia such as the Malay Archipelago, including also the islands of Hawaii and the island of Japan in the Pacific Ocean, and the islands of Andaman, Ceylon, Nicobar, Madagascar, and others in the Indian Ocean. During these voyages the Malays landed and formed countries on the southeastern shores of the continent of Asia.

Some of these Malays continually sailed back and forth, and some of them stayed to settle in those places until they had children, grandchildren, and great-grandchildren who became dwellers in all the places mentioned. As a result, all the islands

10

in the Pacific Ocean and Indian Ocean together with several places on the shores of the mainland of the continent of Asia had settlers who were descendants of the ancient Malays. Thus, also several islands to the west were called the "Malay Archipelago," the archipelago inhabited by Malays who are descended from these ancient ancestors.

There are many places on the shores of the continent of Asia which have at some time been visited and inhabited by ancient Malays, especially in the Malay peninsula which they called Tanah Melayu. Although now some of these places mentioned are no longer settled by Malays, nevertheless from chronicles and history together with the appearances of traces and names of places or villages and so forth, it is clear that in ancient times they were once inhabited by Malays. Some of them are in the northern part of the Malay peninsula, in the area under Siam-Thai control. Many places or villages are still found which are known by Malay names.

In the Siam-Thai annals of Singgora it is noted that at one place on the north coast of the estuary of the country of Singgora on the side of a hill named Kauding or "Red Hill," in the ancient days there existed a country of Malay people. When that country existed and what the name of that country was is not definitely known. It is also believed that perhaps it was this country which originally was called the country of Singgora because the meaning of Singgora is "hill."[19]

Furthermore, we find that the annals of the country of Pattalung say that a raja who ruled that country was of the Islamic religion. His name was Sultan Sulaiman. This Malay kingdom at last was overthrown by its enemies and Sultan Sulaiman died in the battle. Therefore all the people of the country were scattered. Some of them fled north and opened up a new country [also] called Pattalung or Badalung, which today is under the rule of the kingdom of Siam-Thai. The body of the late Sultan Sulaiman was buried in his country. The area of the cemetery still can be seen today. It is full of nothing by jungle. The Malays in Singgora and Nakhon Sri Thammarat call this graveyard "*Hum*", that is "the late."[20] It is still much visited by the residents of that country every year.

11

There is another country called Champa mentioned in books on the history of the people of French Indochina. This country was established by Malays who visited there in ancient times. Their capitol was Indrapura. This country was very famous for its strength from the beginning of the first century A.D., but in A.D. 1471 this country was overthrown by its enemies, the Annamese. It is no longer known where the country of Champa was located. We can only note that it is in history books.[21]

The information cited above has shown how long were the voyages and how great was the spirit of the Malays at that time, who came to rule in the countries of people everywhere. This is very different from the Malays of today.

When the Malays arrived from Sumatera in Malaya, at first they lived only on the seashores and the nearby islands. They passed along the southern shores, afterward gradually entering northern Malaya. Although at that time the Siam-Asli controlled Malaya, nevertheless their power lay in the interior far from the seas because normally the Siam-Asli preferred not to live beside the ocean. Thus it came about that their countries were established in the interior far from the sea.

So it was that when the Malays who came to Malaya stayed only on the fringes of the shore, there were no disputes or enmity with the Siam-Asli since they had their separate places of residence. Also the Malays of that time used customs and religions which were similar to the Siam-Asli and therefore they were able to live peacefully. In fact, the Malays arrived at that time with no intention other than to make a living together in Malaya, but as time passed the number of Malays increased until they inhabited all of Malaya throughout the eastern, western, and southern shores, as well as to the north. Meanwhile, the kingdom of Srivijaya had come to power in Sumatera. Thus the aim of the Malays then changed from that of subsisting to that of taking power in Malaya. This process was begun by one of the princes of Srivijaya named Raja Nila Utama who established the country Tumasik, which had previously been settled by Malays.[22] The kingdom which ruled there came to be called Singapura and this country was the very first to be established by Malays in Malaya. Not many years later the raja of Srivijaya finally subjugated all their countries so that all power of the Siam-Asli in Malaya was shattered.

Now let us briefly consider the situation of the kingdom of Srivijaya. The kingdom of Srivijaya was established by ancient Malays on the island of Sumatera, the first Malay kingdom which held power on that island. Since the first century A.D. its center of government was in modern-day Palembang.[23] The people who developed this country were Malays of the Hindu religion who were also called Hindu Malays.

Their kingdom was ruled by several descendants of their raja, and they were called the descendants of the Rajah Silin.[24] Thus it is also believed that the raja who first established and held the throne of the Srivijaya kingdom was named Raja Silin. It is also said that this raja was a descendent of the family of the "Kings of the Mountain," an indication of the height of their power at that time.[25]

The kingdom of Srivijaya prospered greatly until in the fourteenth century its power was broken. During the time it held power all countries which were governed by the Siam-Asli were completely subjugated including Malaya, Sumatera, Java, Bali, and others. In the eighth century A.D. Srivijaya succeeded in subjugating the country of Malaya and also at the end of that century his majesty subjugated the country of Kedah. Then in the ninth century A.D. the power of Srivijaya increased and spread until his majesty subjugated the country of Nakhon Sri Thammarat together with several countries to the north, including the country of Nakhon Phatung or Nikapatam which is situated on the west side of Bangkok today.

Srivijaya erected large temples in the countries of Nakhon Sri Thammarat and Nakhon Phatung. There are still some of their temples remaining yet today.[26] At that time, the power of the Siam-Asli in Malaya shifted to the Malays from Sumatera. During this time, the Malays freely came to Malaya until they crowded into all of Malaya and developed several countries, first Johor, then Selangor, Trengganu, Perak, Kelantan, and Patani. All these countries submitted to the authority of Srivijaya.

The power of the kingdom of Srivijaya continued to persist and expand until almost the end of the fourth century A.D. Then its power gradually began to weaken because at that time the country of Palembang, the center of its government in Sumatera, fell into the hands of the kingdom of Majapahit, a kingdom newly in power on the island of Java. In the year A.D. 1377 the kingdom of Majapahit subjugated the country of Singapura and all the countries in Malaya.

As the kingdom of Srivijaya gradually began to lose its power, the Thai who had come to inhabit and control Siam began to attack and subjugate the country of Nakhon Sri Thammarat and the countries in southern Siam so that the power of Srivijaya in Malaya and Siam was completely broken. Then Malaya was separated into two parts, the northern part ruled by the Thai kingdom and the southern part dominated by the Majapahit kingdom.

Although all the Malay countries were subject to the Majapahit kingdom, because the center of its government was located on Java, which was very far away from Malaya, the Malay countries were allowed to be ruled by their respective rajas. When the Majapahit kingdom lost power after being subjugated by an Islamic kingdom in Java, more and more matters and affairs in Malaya were neglected. Thereafter the authority to govern returned to the Malay rajas who ruled their respective countries. Since then the Malay rajas have been firmly seated on their royal thrones, free and undisturbed by anyone, the basis for the freedom of the states [negeri] in Malay today.[27]

When the Islamic religion was born in the Arabian Peninsula, brought by the Master Prophet Mohammad, it spread to India, and from India the Islamic religion was brought to Malaya and the islands to the East. Historians have said that Muslims began to settle in the country of Kedah from the ninth century A.D. They were Arab, Indian, and Parsi merchants who came to do business in Malaya.

In the year A.D. 1403 one of the Hindu Malay rajas who ruled over the kingdom of Melaka voluntarily converted to Islam.[28] His majesty in the time of Hinduism was known as Raja Parameswara and when he became a Muslim his majesty was known as Sultan Mahmud Shah. Afterward Raja Mahawangsa, who ruled Kedah, also adopted Islam and was given the title Sultan Mansur Shah. Since then Islam has spread far and wide through all the countries in Malaya and as far as a few territories

14

under the rule of Siam. Thus the Siamese who have adopted Islam are called Samsam.[29]

Chapter 2

THE DEVELOPMENT OF PATANI AND
THE DESCENT OF ITS RAJAS

In time Kedah was developed and became a prosperous country and Singapura and Melaka were developed by Malays who came from the island of Sumatera. In this period the name Patani was not yet known. It is believed that in the area which came to be known as Patani there lived Siam-Asli as it is definitely known that long ago all of Malaya was settled by these peoples. Even so, at that time there were Malays who came from the island of Sumatera and settled on the coasts of Malaya, and some of them gained power and established countries in the south such as Singapura and Melaka. Nevertheless, the influence of the Malays did not yet extend to the north. The Siam-Asli continued to control the north of Malaya, in Pahang, Kedah, Kelantan, and thus also in Patani. All of the governments of the Siam-Asli were under the protection of the center of their government which was established at Ligor or Nakhon Sri Thammarat.

At this time in Patani there was established a kingdom of Siam-Asli the center of whose rule was located in the district of Perawan, although the actual name of the country is not known.[*]

---

[*]Now called Kampung Perawan situated in the district of Jering. Its official name is "Krung" which in the Siamese language mans city or citadel of the raja [*Kota Raja*]. In this village there still exists the ruins of the Kota Raja and traces of antiquity which were erected by the Siam-Asli. There also is a large Buddhist idol in a cave on top of a hill which is revered by Buddhists in the District of Yala yet today. This idol was made by the Siam-Asli and there is evidence which indicates that this figure was made during the same period that Maharaja Srivijaya

17

The stories concerning Patani say only that it was called "Kota Mahligai."[*30] From its traces, still clearly visible, this country was large and was ruled by a number of rajas and eventually was ruled by a raja known in the time of his reign as Raja Sri Wangsa.[**31] At Kota Mahligai there were Malays who came from countries which were recently established in the south of Malaya and also from the island of Sumatera. They came and resided on the coasts by the sea. The country of Kota Mahligai was situated very far inland, some tens of miles from the sea, because the Siam-Asli did not like living near the sea. Because of this, Kota Mahligai only with difficulty was reached by traders and merchants, causing the prosperity and luxury of Kota Mahligai to decrease with each day. Finally the inhabitants of the country gradually were forced to leave and make a living outside of the country's capital. As Kota Mahligai began to lose its inhabitants, the villages newly founded by Malays near the sea became more developed and populated because merchant boats began to stop and sell their goods there. Among the merchants were some who chose to stay, working and trading in that place so that it became prosperous and densely populated.

Palembang erected the pillars of the sanctuary at Ligor. In view of the traces still present it is believed that the kingdom of the Siam-Asli in Patani was long established and was not insignificant.

[*]The name is still a matter of confusion because the word Mahligai is from the Persian language, not from the Siamese or Hindu languages. It is possible also that writers of books concerning Patani have been mistaken in taking this word from "maha nikaya" which means country of followers of the Mahayana sect of Buddhism. It also can be understood from the translation of the Pra Wang to mean Kota Raja which then was called Kota Mahligai. In this matter it is not yet certain which [interpretation] is correct.

[**]The name of this raja is written in a book of stories on Patani as "Paya korp Mahyana," meaning raja who worships the Mahayana religion. This was not his official name. In the words of the Malay Annals it is stated that the name of the raja who first opened up the country of Patani was Raja Sri Bangsa or Sri Wangsa. This writer is of the opinion that the name Sri Wangsa is more accurate.

18

At that time on the coast of the country of Patani a village was established and first settled by an old Malay fisherman named "Tani." This old man was very well-mannered and refined and he became the head of the group of fishermen there. The inhabitants of that village honored and praised him, and he was given the title of Bapak, and called "Pak Tani."[32] That village increased in population day by day until finally it was called Kampung Pak Tani [Village of Pak Tani].

This village was situated in a very beautiful area with level land high above the floods of the rainy season. Its coast formed a wide bay while in front of it extended a long cape, so that within the bay there was a very good harbor for boats and ships, well protected from the danger of waves and heavy winds. The fishermen in Kampung Pak Tani were able to catch fish and other marine life in the bay without having to go far into the middle of the sea. Within the area of the high and level land, the inhabitants of Kampung Pak Tani worked their wet rice fields. Near their village there was a small river by which boats could easily go to and from the sea, known today as the Kerisik River. Because of this it was not long before Kampung Pak Tani became large and its inhabitants numerous. It became a large city while on the coast there was a trading center for merchants who regularly came to the city.

As Kampung Pak Tani grew increasingly large, Kota Mahligai became more and more lonely because many of its inhabitants left. Finally Raja Sri Wangsa decided to move from the capital of the country. He moved with all of the royal family and common people, and erected a large palace near Kampung Pak Tani in the District of Kerisik. This royal citadel [kota istana] was built across the river facing Kampung Pak Tani. The entrance of the royal citadel faced the river to facilitate traffic by boat. This river was named the Papiri River, not Parit River as it is known today. (The Papiri River has since been filled in.)

As soon as the royal citadel was completed, his majesty ordered the excavation of a moat around the citadel as a defense against attacks by enemies, according to the defensive strategies of that era. The moat was dug beginning from the Kerisik River proceeding behind his majesty's citadel until it rejoined with the

Papiri River at Kampung Parit. Raja Sri Wangsa together with all his royal family and commoners settled within the royal citadel of Kampung Kerisik, and Kota Mahligai was abandoned.

At that time the place where the royal citadel was built by Raja Sri Wangsa had not yet been named, but because it was situated near Kampung Pak Tani most people simply called it the country of Pak Tani. Then it began to be known by the name of "Pak Tani." Thus the Arabs who came to trade at Patani also called it "Patani" as that was easier for them to pronounce.[33] Then Patani began to be known throughout the world, East and West, and became the subject of several fantastic and remarkable tales from the past until this day.

After Raja Sri Wangsa was established as the ruler of Patani, the country became even more populous and trading progressed due to visits by merchants from other countries. Several years later Raja Sri Wangsa died and he was replaced on the throne of Patani by his son who was named Raja Intera (Indra).[34]

The raja in power and all of the commoners in Patani continued to follow the religion introduced by the Hindus, the Buddhist religion of the Mahayana sect. At the same time on the island of Sumatera there existed a country named Pasai whose residents had embraced the Islamic religion, but surrounding their country there were still many people of the Hindu religion. Therefore, the country of Pasai was frequently attacked by the Hindus causing the Muslims in the country of Pasai to endure a life of hardship. Some of them left for other countries to save themselves. Among them there were those who fled in the direction of Patani, so that Patani began to receive Muslims arriving from Pasai. They built a village there, all the residents of which were people from Pasai, and the village was named Kampung Pasai, as it is today.

Among the Pasai Muslims there was an old man learned in religious law named Sheik Syafialudin. This old man was also known as a *dukun* skilled in treating many different illnesses.[35] Because of this the residents of Patani honored and were exceedingly respectful toward the Tuan Sheik.[36]

At one time Raja Intera (Raja Patani) was afflicted by a disease which broke out over his body, leprosy. The longer it

20

lasted the worse it became. Many dukun and healers of the Siam-Asli were called to treat his majesty but to no avail. Then his majesty ordered his servant to beat a cymbal throughout the country to find someone able to treat his majesty's disease, offering several gifts. The raja's servant traveled while striking the cymbal through every village and field looking for a dukun able to treat his majesty's illness but without success until he entered the village of the people of Pasai. When Sheik Syafialudin heard the striking of the cymbal he went out and asked, "Why do you strike that cymbal?" Replied the raja's servant, "Our raja is afflicted with leprosy, every one of the dukun in the country has tried to treat it without success. Because of this I walk striking the cymbal looking for someone who is able to treat his majesty's illness, and his majesty has promised to give a fine gift to the one able to treat him." Then said Sheik Syafialudin, "Tell your raja I am able to treat his disease."

Several days later Sheik Syafialudin was seen coming to the royal citadel and entered into the presence of His Majesty Raja Intera. When his majesty inquired whether it was true that Tuan Sheik was able to treat his disease, respectfully he replied, "Your will be done, Your Majesty, a thousand pardons, your humble servant is willing to treat it, but with the stipulation that Your Majesty will make a vow to your humble servant first." His majesty said, "What promises do you want?" Answered Sheik Syafialudin, "It is the wish of your humble servant that should your Sovereign Majesty's disease be cured by our humble servant, Your Majesty would be willing to leave behind the Buddhist religion and follow that of your humble servant, the Islamic religion." The wish of Sheik Syafialudin was granted by his majesty. After several days his majesty's disease was cured by the Tuan Sheik. So exceedingly happy was his majesty that he bestowed much property upon Sheik Syafialudin. But his majesty's promise to change his religion was not fulfilled.

It was not long thereafter that his majesty's disease again recurred. His majesty ordered that Sheik Syafialudin be called to treat him once again. Sheik Syafialudin agreed to treat him but with the condition already noted to which the raja must submit. After treating him for several days the disease was cured. Again his majesty disavowed the wishes of the sheik and the disease

21

returned for a third time. It was again ordered that Sheik Syafialudin treat him. This time Sheik Syafialudin came respectfully to the raja saying, "As long as Your Majesty does not fulfill Your Majesty's promises to your humble servant, during that time Your Majesty's disease will not be cured." Upon hearing the words of the Sheik, his majesty commanded, "Cure my disease this time and I will be obliged to fulfill my promises." Then Sheik Syafialudin once again treated his majesty's illness until finally it was cured, and after that his majesty's body was restored.

After this his majesty invited Sheik Syafialudin into this palace and ordered him to teach the confession of faith. Sheik Syafialudin was extremely pleased knowing that his desire was achieved, and taught his majesty how to pronounce the confession of faith. Since that time his majesty firmly embraced the Islamic faith and turned away from the Buddhist religion.

At the behest of Raja Intera, Sheik Syafialudin was appointed to teach Islamic law in his palace and he was given the elevated title of "Datuk Sri Raja Patih," Thus Datuk Sri Raja Patih continued teaching Islamic law to his majesty, the royal family, and other important people until they too embraced the Islamic religion. After this the Islamic religion began to spread beyond the royal palace and was accepted by the common people of Patani as well. Finally, all the people of Patani embraced the religion of Islam, and the Hindu religion gradually began to weaken as the people of Patani no longer paid it any attention. Buddhist idols and places of worship were completely collapsed and destroyed.[37]

Since that time the people of Patani have followed the religion of Islam, which until this day has become their national religion. One day Datuk Sri Raja Patih convened a public gathering to install Raja Intera as sultan according to Islamic customs, giving his majesty the title Sultan Mahmud Shah. Then the titles of all the raja's chief men were arranged according to the style of titles which are used in Malay countries, titles for the rank of their ministers being called datuk and orang kaya, so that those titles were soon restricted [to only those people holding certain offices].

When matters within the country were thus settled, Sultan Mahmud Shah composed a missive to foreign lands to be carried by a party of his ambassadors to the sultan of Melaka to strengthen the bonds of friendship between the two countries, especially as Melaka was known as the oldest Malay country and the first to embrace Islam. At that time the sultan who ruled Melaka was Sultan Mahmud Shah.* When the ambassadors from the Malay kingdom of Patani arrived in Melaka they were greeted by the sultan of Melaka with full honors. When the ambassadors returned to Patani many things were sent as gifts to the sultan of Patani.

Not many years thereafter Sultan Mahmud Shah [of Patani] sent a mission to the country of Siam, which was ruled from Ayuthia, in order to form friendly ties between his majesty and the Siam-Thai raja.** After that Patani became increasingly known to the outside world so that its name was recognized by all the Eastern and Western peoples. Even more than during the time of his majesty's father, merchants began to gather in Patani, selling and buying their wares. They included Siam-Thai, Chinese, Japanese, Javanese, Indians, and Arabs. Only the Europeans had not yet arrived at Patani.

Each day Patani increased in populousness while the trading between peoples continually progressed. The mouth of the Patani River was constantly frequented by ships which carried trade goods from foreign lands so that the development of Patani at that time was no less than that of Melaka, which was older. Development in Patani continued until the year A.D. 1516, the century of the arrival of the European peoples in East Asia. In that year Patani first received a Portuguese ship arriving from Melaka carrying many different kinds of trade goods with the intention of trading in the country of Patani. By that time Melaka had been subjugated by the Portuguese. When the Portuguese ship arrived at

---

*Ascending to the throne of the kingdom of Melaka in the year A.D. 1478, his majesty was the last sultan to govern the country of Malacca. In the year 1511 Melaka was subjugated by the Portuguese.

**At that time the country of Siam was under the control of the Siam-Thai. At first their center of administration was in Sukothai; subsequently their center of government was moved to Ayuthia.

Kuala Patani, its captain landed on the beach and came before his majesty asking permission to trade within Patani. This request was for a factory for their trade in the city of Patani. This was the first visit of the European peoples to Patani, and the Portuguese were the first who came to trade in Patani.

The arrival of the Portuguese in East Asia was solely for the purpose of trade.[38] On the continent of Europe they had established a trading company whose purpose was to expand their trade in the eastern region. Early in the fifteenth century A.D. Portuguese trading ships began to sail for India. From there they first heard of the fame of Melaka's commerce. When they saw that Melaka's location was very favorable from a commercial standpoint, even better than they had dreamed, and that internal commerce was well developed, an imperialistic spirit arose among the Portuguese, who desired to govern Melaka themselves. Therefore in April of A.D. 1511 there arrived a force of Portuguese war ships captained by Alphonso d'Alberquerque, who attacked and landed his troops in the beach of Melaka. A fierce battle with the people of Melaka took place, but the defenses of the city of Melaka, which were regarded as being invincible, were successfully destroyed and the country of Melaka fell into the hands of the Portuguese. Melaka then became a center for Portuguese trade in Southeast Asia. The Portuguese then began to send their trading ships to Patani.

In Patani the trade of the Portuguese steadily increased because at that time there were no other European peoples conducting trade there and they were able to do so freely. One trade item that the Portuguese brought, which was exceedingly remarkable in the eyes of the Patani Malays, was firearms, that is, guns and their bullets. The Patani Malays were not yet acquainted with these weapons. Only when they were brought by the Portuguese did they learn and master their use. After that time trading ships and Portuguese flocked to trade in Patani.

A Portuguese merchant named Pinto who came to trade in Patani in the year A.D. 1538 wrote in his diary as follows: "At the time I arrived in Patani in that year, I met nearly 300 Portuguese who lived within the city of Patani. Besides these Portuguese there were also Eastern peoples such as Siam-Thai, Chinese, and Japanese. The Japanese commerce is very extensive in this city."[39]

Information found in books on Patani's history indicates that His Majesty Sultan Mahmud Shah, who then occupied the throne of the Malay kingdom of Patani, always governed justly, causing the country of Patani gradually to increase the level of its development. Several years thereafter his majesty died leaving two sons, that is Raja Muzafar and Raja Mansur, together with one daughter named Raja Aisyah. Raja Aisyah married Raja Jalalludin who governed the country of Sai.

With the agreement of the royal family and the chiefs, Raja Muzafar was proclaimed sultan to replace his father the late Sultan Mahmud Shah, and he was given the title Sultan Muzafar Shah. His younger brother, Raja Mansur was appointed *Raja Muda* while his majesty appointed the grandchild of Datuk Sri Raja Patih to become one of his chiefs, as was to be the case from generation to generation.[40]

After Sultan Muzafar Shah had occupied the throne of the kingdom of Patani for some time, his majesty considered visiting the country of Siam-Thai in order to make acquaintances and to create a closer friendship with that country's raja. As soon as preparations had been completed his majesty temporarily turned over the government of the country to his younger brother, Raja Mansur. Then his majesty set sail with several ships escorted by his chiefs and their soldiers in the direction of the country of Siam-Thai. After several days' sail his majesty arrived at the mouth of the Chao Phrya River, that is the estuary of the country of Siam. By following this river his majesty's expedition proceeded upstream straight to the city of Ayuthia.* His majesty was not well received by the raja of Siam-Thai because the raja of Siam-Thai considered the rank of his majesty very much lower than his own. After his majesty had stayed there but a few days, his majesty returned to Patani with a feeling of grievance and dissatisfaction aroused by the proud nature of the Siam-Thai. When his majesty departed, the raja of Siam-Thai gave him several slaves from his prisoners of war, people of Pegu (Burma) and people of Khmer

---

*This was the center of the Thai government once they gained control of the country of Siam. Its raja was named Phra Maha Cakkraphat. [He reigned between 1548 and 1568/69.]

(Cambodia). All the captive slaves were brought back to Patani and his majesty gave them a village in which to live. To this day their descendants are still to be found in that village. Because those people were still of the Buddhist religion, a monastery was built within their village which was named Kedi, meaning monk's house. Because of this, the Malays of Patani named that village Kampung Kedi, and so it has remained until this day.

In the year A.D. 1563 there came to Sultan Muzafar Shah the news that the country of Siam was under attack by the Burmese. His majesty remembered the proud nature of the Siam-Thai which had been shown during the time of his majesty's visit to the city of Ayuthia. His majesty met in council with his younger brother and his chiefs and a decision was reached to attack Ayuthia as repayment for their shame and to take revenge upon the Siam-Thai. His younger brother, Raja Mansur, together with all ministers and war chiefs agreed to accompany his majesty to war.

Then his majesty commanded the preparation of 200 warships, one thousand soldiers, and 100 women as a combined force led by his majesty to attack Siam. Several days later the army departed from Patani and headed for the country of the Siam-Thai, while the government of the country was left to one of his majesty's chiefs. Then his majesty sailed with his army to Siam-Thai.

When Sultan Muzafar Shah arrived with his army at Siam-Thai he discovered that the citadel of Ayuthia was surrounded by Burmese soldiers. Quickly his majesty landed his army and immediately invaded the royal citadel of Siam-Thai, running amuck and killing the Siamese until the Siam-Thai, who were guarding the front of the citadel, were killed by the Patani Malay soldiers.[41] Finally, all the defenses of the Siam-Thai were weakened, and one by one they fled. At that time their raja was within his palace. When he heard the war cries of the Malay soldiers, who had successfully seized the citadel's gate, he fled through a door in the back of the citadel and ran to hide in a place named "Maha Phram Island." There the Siam-Thai regathered their strength to counter-attack the army of Patani Malays.

As soon as they were sated with running amuck and killing the Siam-Thai, the Malay army left the citadel, returned to their ships, and immediately weighed their anchors to sail back to Patani. But when their army had gone as far as the mouth of the Chao Phrya River, by the will of God who is all powerful, His Majesty Sultan Muzafar Shah suddenly died, and they were forced to bury him at the estuary of the country of Siam. The army returned to Patani with sadness at the loss of their beloved raja.

At the time that Sultan Muzafar Shah set out to attack Siam, his queen was pregnant. After his majesty died and Raja Mansur had returned to Patani the queen had not yet given birth. There arose a question as to who should be elevated to the throne of the late sultan. At that time there was an older son of his majesty named Raja Mambang, a child borne by a concubine. According to royal prescripts, offspring from a concubine may not be elevated to become sultan. Because of this the entire royal family and all of the chiefs decided that Raja Mansur would become sultan and be given the title Sultan Mansur Shah.

As soon as the ceremony inaugurating Raja Mansur was completed, the queen of the late sultan gave birth to a son who was named Raja Patik Siam, to obtain good fortune from the death of his father in Siam.[42] Not long thereafter word came of the death of Raja Jelal, ruler of the country of Sai and husband of Raja Aisyah, and that he had died without leaving a single child. Sultan Mansur Shah elevated one of his chiefs to govern that country and invited Raja Aisyah to return and reside with his majesty in Patani.

For nine years Sultan Mansur Shah occupied the throne of the Malay kingdom of Patani. When he died he left two sons, Raja Bahadur and Raja Bima, a child borne by a concubine. Before he died, his majesty made a will to the effect that should his majesty die it was his wish that Raja Patik Siam, the son of his brother, be inaugurated sultan. This was carried out by Raja Aisyah, his aunt, who became regent.

There was also Raja Mambang, elder brother of the sultan. When he saw that his younger brother had become sultan he felt envy, hate and dissatisfaction towards his younger brother. He was constantly incited by his comrades until his hatred could not longer be contained. Thus one day while it was still morning, just at the break of dawn, while Sultan Patik Siam was praying alone within the palace, Raja Mambang entered that room with a drawn dagger [*keris*] intending to murder the sultan from behind.

Seeing this, Raja Aisyah realized Raja Mambang's intent and ran to embrace the sultan to protect him so that he would not be stabbed by Raja Mambang. But at that moment Raja Mambang lost his senses and, following the impulse of a passionate heart, immediately stabbed both intertwined bodies without pity. Sultan Patik Siam, together with his aunt Raja Aisyah, fell in the middle of the palace chamber completely smeared with blood and in but a moment both were dead.

The palace was shaken by word that the sultan and Raja Aisyah had been murdered by Raja Mambang. All of the raja's people gathered to look for Raja Mambang within the palace, surrounded Raja Mambang in a chamber, and stabbed him with a lance. Raja Mambang died before he was able to flee the palace.

After Sultan Patik Siam died, the royal family and chiefs agreed to elevate Raja Bahadur, son of the late Sultan Mansur Shah, to become sultan, and he was given the name Sultan Bahadur Shah. For many years his majesty sat upon the throne of the kingdom until one day there occurred a dispute between his majesty and his elder brother, Raja Bima. This dispute became increasingly heated until it caused Raja Bima to become unfaithful to his majesty.

The contentious atmosphere became grimmer with the passing of each day and finally resulted in a saddening incident. One day, as his majesty was praying within his palace, Raja Bima entered quietly and stealthily, then quickly stabbed his majesty from behind so that his dagger disappeared in his majesty's stomach. His majesty fell forward without a chance to fight. In a moment his majesty was died. Similarly Raja Bima, before he could run away, was surrounded by his majesty's people and he too in turn was stabbed until he died. At his death Sultan Bahadur Shah left behind three daughters, but no sons. The daughters were named Raja Hijau, Raja Biru, and Raja Ungu [Green Princess, Blue Princess, and Purple Princess].

In a council meeting among the royal family and the chiefs, a decision was made to elevate Raja Hijau to ascend the throne of the kingdom of Patani, the very first female Raja to rule the country of Patani.

For many years Raja Hijau governed with feminine justice and skill. Her name became famous in all countries including the continent of Europe, so that rajas of those countries sent missions to Patani in order to strengthen bonds of friendship. Raja Hijau also sent missions to the rajas of those countries to return their expressions of friendship. Among them were the rajas of Siam and Japan. This is known from the information provided by Pinto, the Portuguese merchant, who stated that earlier there were Japanese who came to trade in Patani but that their raja had not yet established official ties of friendship with the kingdom of Patani. Only during the reign of the female Raja did the raja of Japan begin to take notice and send his envoys to Patani requesting official permissions to trade in Patani.

In the history of the Japanese people it is said that in the year A.D. 1592 there set sail a ship from Japan carrying a letter from their raja together with many kinds of gifts to the raja of Patani and requesting official permission for Japanese to conduct trade in Patani. The raja of Japan's mission was well received by the raja of Patani and all of its requests were granted.

Seven years later, that is in the year A.D. 1599, the raja of Patani sent a mission to Japan to appear before their raja to secure ties of friendship, and a second mission was sent in the year A.D. 1606. Each time the missions of the raja of Patani arrived they were well received by the raja of Japan. Afterwards commercial relations between Patani and Japan steadily increased.

At that time the largest center of commerce in Japan was the country of "Birado" which was situated near the territory of present-day Nagasaki. From that country Japanese trading ships carried their trade goods to Patani. These ships sailed back and forth without interruption.

Thus also relations with Siam became increasingly close because Siam was very close to the country of Patani. Trading ships continually came and went and crowds of Siam-Thai came to trade in Patani. Thus also the people of Patani frequently traded in Siam. The Raja of Patani and the Raja of Siam-Thai regularly sent missions in order to enhance friendly relationships.

In all communications the raja of Siam-Thai always referred to the raja of Patani by the title of Pra Nang Chau Ying, meaning her majesty the female Raja. This title over time became permanent so that the female rajas who occupied the throne of the kingdom of Patani after Raja Hijau were always referred to by this title by the raja of Siam. This title became increasingly well known so that the Malays of Patani themselves called their raja in accordance with what she was called by the Raja of Siam. But because of the accent of the Malays, this title Pra Nang Chau Ying was pronounced Raja Nang Chayang. This title continued to be used by all of the female rajas who governed the country of Patani.

During the time that Raja Hijau occupied the throne of the kingdom of Patani the country became increasingly developed and populous. Her majesty was exceedingly conscientious concerning the problems of her populace. One of the works that her majesty performed was the digging of a river. At that time the Kerisik River which flowed in the midst of the common people was almost useless because the water was brackish and it did not go far inland. All the wet rice fields there could not produce a good crop because of the brackish water. Thus one day her majesty called upon the corvée laborers and gathered all of her people to extend the river beginning from the Kerisik River proceeding inland until it joined the Sungai Besar [Big River] at Kuala Temangan (at the present-day fort of Kampung Perigi). As soon as it joined the Sungai Besar, the water came down following the river that was excavated and swiftly poured into the Kerisik River and then into the sea at Kuala Ru. With the arrival of the water from upstream, the water in the Kerisik River became fresh and all of the wet rice fields were able to produce satisfactorily.[*]

While Patani was governed by Raja Hijau its name became well-known and famous throughout the world, East and West. Its harbor was always full of the trading ships of several peoples. The Dutch also came to conduct their commerce in Patani and became the second European people after the Portuguese.

---

[*]Later the excavated river was filled in again by Raja Biru and the brackish water returned once again.

The Dutch arrived in East Asia after they learned of the success of Portuguese commerce in Asia, which produced exceedingly good profits. Wishing to share in the profits of the Portuguese, the Dutch were inspired to form a trading company to carry out trade in Asia. The Dutch began to send trading ships to Asia, and the country of India became their first goal. From India the Dutch first came to Malaya. The arrival of the Dutch caused a feeling of dissatisfaction among the Portuguese, who felt that it would disturb the basis of their trade with the Asian peoples. With time, this feeling became increasingly strong, finally resulting in a dispute between the two peoples, each of whom endeavored to gain power in every aspect of trade. The Portuguese began to take steps to block all progress in trade by the Dutch.

The Dutch conducted their trade without heeding the actions of the Portuguese until in the year A.D. 1641, Melaka, which had been ruled by the Portuguese and had become the center for their trade, was attacked by the Dutch. The battle between the two European peoples over Melaka was violent, and in that year Melaka fell into the hands of the Dutch, causing the commercial power of the Portuguese to decline and their influence in Malaya to crode. Finally all of their relationships with Malaya were eliminated by the Dutch. After that the Dutch began to establish a relationship with the Kingdom of Patani.

One day, in the year A.D. 1602, a Dutch trading ship suddenly entered the harbor of Patani, captained by Daniel van de Leck. As soon as the ship dropped anchor, the captain landed and entered the palace of the raja, coming before the raja of Patani with gifts and requesting permission that the Dutch might conduct their trade in Patani. Her majesty granted this request. At this all of the Dutch landed and built a factory for their trade. The entry of the Dutch to Patani was very alarming to the Japanese and Portuguese. A feeling of hate towards the Dutch was implanted in the hearts of the Japanese and Portuguese, but because they did not have the chance to oppose the Dutch they were forced to remain silent for several years.

At that time Patani had reached such a high level of progress and prosperity that it would be difficult to find Malay countries comparable to Patani. A German traveler named

31

Mandelslohe had the opportunity to visit Patani during that period. In his diary he wrote:

> Patani is a very prosperous country. The people of Patani are able to eat fruits of scores of different kinds each month. Chickens here lay eggs twice each day. The paddy is exceedingly plentiful, there are many kinds of meat such as beef, mutton, goose, duck, chicken, capon, peacock, deer jerky, mouse-deer, and birds, together with hundreds of kinds of fruits.

Thus the words written by a German traveler demonstrate how prosperous was Patani during that period. In matters of commerce it is also believed that at that time Patani had become an important center of trade within Southeast Asia so that Ayuthia, the center of government of Siam during that period, could not equal the commercial progress of Patani. Seeing the progress of Patani, the raja of Siam was inspired with intense desire to subjugate Patani.

The intensity of the desire of the raja of Siam-Thai to subjugate Patani grew hotter and hotter until in the year A.D. 1603 a Siam-Thai navy from Ayuthia set off toward Patani with thousands of soldiers led by a commander named Okya Decho, who intended to rob the Malays of Patani of their independence and subjugate them.[43] At this time the kingdom of Siam-Thai was governed by a raja who was named "Phraya Naresuan."[44] This raja is very famous in the history of the Siam-Thai people and sought to expand the subjugated territories and to destroy the independence of other peoples.

When the Siam-Thai navy reached Patani, the Siamese commander began to land his troops at Kuala Patani and launched an invasion. The people of Patani under the leadership of their Raja came out to fight off the attack of the Siam-Thai. With full assistance from the merchants within Patani, including the Europeans, who gave assistance with firearms, cannon, and materials, they fought the aggression of the Siam-Thai. The people of Patani used cannon to bombard the Siam-Thai until they were weakened, landing further away because many of their soldiers were killed and wounded. Finally the Siam-Thai retreated to their ships and set sail for home, having suffered a terrible defeat.

When they arrived at Ayuthia the raja of Siam began to realize the importance of cannon in war. Several years later he sent a mission to Patani to buy cannon, because at that time these weapons were very plentiful in Patani and their sale became an important business. The raja of Japan also desired these cannon which were purchased from Patani.

In the national history of Japan it is written that in the year A.D. 1606 the raja of Japan sent a mission to the raja of Siam at Ayuthia asking the help of this raja to purchase cannon and send them to his country. Another mission was sent in the direction of India. There the English began to learn of the fame and progress of the commerce within Patani.

On the fifth of January A.D. 1611 a trading ship named The Globe left from London, captained by Anthony Heath, and carrying numerous trade goods together with gifts from his raja, in addition to a letter which was to be delivered to the female raja of Patani. This ship sailed for months in the direction of the continent of Asia, making short stops until on the 23rd of June A.D. 1611 this ship arrived at Patani. Her captain landed and came before the female raja of Patani carrying gifts and the letter from his raja, together with a request for permission from her majesty to allow the English to trade in Patani. Permission was granted by her majesty just as she had favored each of the other European peoples.

The people of Patani greeted the arrival of the English with gladness, but as for the Dutch, Portuguese, and others, the feeling of dissatisfaction was very strong and increasingly they hated the English. After the ship The Globe had been anchored at Patani a month the English built a trading factory to store their trade goods. After that the English began to trade in Patani.

Among the Englishmen who came with the ship The Globe was an English merchant named Peter Will Peloris. He wrote concerning his travels to Patani:

> On the first of June in the year A.D. 1611 we departed
> from Bintam (on the island of Java) and sailed to
> Patani. We arrived at Patani on the 22nd of that

33

June.[45]   We asked for news from people who were in a ship in the harbor concerning the customs and traditions of the inhabitants. On the 26th of June we landed, carrying a letter and gifts to the female raja of Patani. There we were greeted by an honor guard. Then we were brought into the city. The letter from our raja was received and placed on top of a small golden piece of gauze and then carried by an elephant into the city.

The palace of the female raja was beautifully constructed. We received permission from her majesty to trade within Patani, just as do the Dutch. We returned from the palace of the raja without being able to come before her majesty herself, but her people brought us to the house of one of her chiefs who is named "Orang Kaya Sri Nuna."[*] The next day we were favored by her majesty with many kinds of fruits ordered to be sent to our ship by her people.

On the third of July of that year a Dutch ship named Lipri Thim left Patani for Japan. We sent a letter with that ship to Mister Adams who traded in Japan. We planned to request permission from the raja of Patani to build a trading factory within Patani but we had to expend not a little expense for this matter.

In the time we stayed at Patani many people on our ship were afflicted by a disease. Mister Heath, captain of our ship, also was afflicted by this disease, and on the ninth of July he died. We selected Mister Brown to become captain, but Mister Brown also died of his disease, and we had to select Mister Thomas Eppington to replace him as well. Since then we have had increasingly ill luck. Many of our trade goods have been stolen. Nearly 280 bolts of cloth have been stolen from my box.

---

[*]It is believed that his name was Orang Kayo Inche Yunus, so it is said in the history of Patani.

There are fifteen people within our house and at night a light is always lit until dawn. I suspect that the thief is none other than one of us because a large dog which we have had here all the time has never sounded a bark. I together with six friends was ordered to remain with the trade goods at Patani until the first of August and the ship The Globe set sail for Siam.

Our commerce in Patani was not very successful and I wished to open a factory for textile trade in the country of Makassar on the island of Celebes. Because of this, on the eighth of October I sent Mister John France to take goods there with a ship. On the next day, 9 October, we received word from Mister Eppington and his followers who went to the country of Siam saying [here what is written concerns only the country of Siam].[46]

We stayed in Patani until the end of the cold season and on 31 December the female raja of Patani departed to play at sea accompanied by 600 boats.[47] On the 25th of January in the year 1612 we received word from Siam saying that our trade goods there had more than half been sold, the largest part being bought by the raja of Siam-Thai himself. Because of this, in the month of March we sent a ship to the country of Ayuthia to take additional goods there.

On 31 July 1612 the sultan of Pahang arrived at Patani. We were invited by the female raja of Patani on the first of August to witness the wedding ceremony of this sultan with the youngest sister of her majesty. We were informed of the reasons for which this marriage was to take place. Her majesty wished to marry her younger sister to the sultan of Pahang, so her majesty sent a mission to the sultan of Pahang to discuss this matter and to invite the sultan of Pahang to visit Patani in order to observe the countenance of her younger sister. But the sultan of Pahang refused to accept her majesty's invitation. Because of this her majesty was extremely angry with the sultan of Pahang as her wish was not granted. Then it was ordered to prepare an army totalling four thousand men and eighty boats to go to Pahang in order to threaten the sultan so that he would agree to marry her younger sister. Truly at that time the country of Pahang was in difficulties. Seeing the army from Patani, the sultan of Pahang was frightened that his country would be laid to waste. So the sultan of Pahang agreed to the wishes of the female raja of Patani and he departed for Patani and the marriage was carried out.

On 21 October in the year 1613 we all decided to return to England and we went before the female raja to inform her of our wish. After we made our request to her majesty, the female raja bestowed upon Captain Eppington a dagger [*keris*]. Then we returned to the ship The Globe and sailed to Masulipatum in India.

This is all that is written in the traveler's tale of an English merchant who came to Patani during the reign of Her Majesty Raja Hijau. His writings serve as an important memoir, portraying the progress and power of the Malay kingdom of Patani at the end of the sixteenth century which is properly commemorated by the Malays of Patani to this day.

The younger sister of Raja Hijau who married the sultan of Pahang was Raja Ungu. After the marriage the sultan returned to Pahang, taking Raja Ungu with him. After that the kingdom of Patani was secure in progress and fame. All of the people lived peacefully and securely, undisturbed by their enemies. After the return of the ship The Globe to England, Patani became increasingly well known among English merchants. Other English ships and merchants regularly came to trade at Patani.

The clearest evidence of this is stated in a history book on Patani which says that early in the seventeenth century Patani's harbor was visited by trading ships from several peoples and became a port of call for ships which came from the country of Surati (in India), Goa, and from the Coromandel coast, and became known as an excellent harbor by the sailing ships that came from the countries of China and Japan.

Meanwhile the feeling of envy and hate among the European merchants who traded in Patani became increasingly intense, especially the feeling of the Dutch against the English. At that time the Dutch had succeeded in taking control of the majority of trade centers in the island of Java. Because of this, the Dutch developed a strong desire to control all of the commercial affairs throughout East Asia for the benefit of their people alone. They began to implement a restrictive policy to reduce and exterminate the trading endeavors of other peoples, especially the English. Because of this, disputes frequently occurred between these people and there arose enmity on both land and sea. Dutch ships, whenever they met with ships owned by the English, always attacked and fired upon them so that in all the eastern seas battles often occurred between Dutch and English ships. Each time these battles occurred the English ships usually were the ones which suffered losses.

With matters in this state, it was difficult for the English to conduct their trade in the East. The officials of the English Company met in council to find ways to protect their trading endeavors and prevent interference by the Dutch. The decision of this meeting was that merchant ships owned by the English Company were to be equipped with weapons in order to fight off enemy attacks. After that time all English merchant ships were changed to resemble the warships of the government.

In the year A.D. 1618, battles due to trade competition frequently occurred between the ships of the Dutch and the English. At Patani, two English merchant ships of the English Company named Simpson and Hound, full of trade goods bound for the country of Champa in Indochina, arrived at Patani on 17 July A.D. 1619, and dropped anchor. At that time Dutch ships were on guard there. When the English ships were seen coming to anchor the Dutch ships quickly attacked and loosed a terrific barrage on the two English ships. The firing startled all of the inhabitants of the city of Patani. The battle lasted five hours before it ended. The ships of the English Company sustained heavy damage and finally raised a flag of surrender and all of the property and trade goods within those ships was seized by the Dutch. The English were captured and the two ships burned.

With this naval victory the Dutch became increasingly bold and their hatred for the English burned hotter. Crowds of Dutchmen landed and began to mistreat the Englishmen in the city of Patani. But Her Majesty Raja Hijau did not permit them to do this; on the contrary she ordered her majesty's people to guard strongly the security of the English. The Dutch were afraid to violate the sovereignty of her majesty. When they met with Englishmen they could only threaten them with swords.

Because the ships of the English Company repeatedly suffered losses due to the actions of the Dutch, the officers of the Company decided to stop their trade within the countries of Patani, Siam, and Japan for the time begin. Beginning in the year A.D. 1623 all Englishmen within the city of Patani left to conduct trade within other countries. From that time relations between the English and Patani ceased, while on the other hand the position of the Dutch within Patani became increasingly strong and they continued their trade freely until their colony on the island of Java was firmly under their control. Only then did the Dutch move their center of trade there [that is to Java]. However, their contacts with Patani continued for some time afterwards.

Time passed, the days rolled by, and several years later Her Majesty Raja Hijau, ruler of the kingdom of Patani, died. Her majesty was given the title Marhum Ketemangan by her people in memory of her majesty's processions to visit her people digging the river at Kampung Temangan.

With the passing of her majesty, the royal household and their chiefs decided to elevate her younger sister Raja Biru to the throne of the kingdom of Patani. Three years later the river that had been dug from Kampung Temangan to Kerisik during the reign of her elder sister, the late Raja Hijau, had begun to flow too swiftly and constantly caused the bank of the river at the foot of the palace to cave in. Moreover, because the water in the Kerisik River had become fresh, all the salt fields at the beach by the river mouth no longer formed salt. The water was not briny enough. Because of this, Her Majesty Raja Biru ordered the construction of a dam to divert the water from the Kerisik River and close off the mouth of the Papiri River. This dam was built with stone and to this day its site of construction is named

Kampung Tahanduk Batu [Stone Dam Village]. Finally the river that had been dug dried up, as did the Papiri River.

Several years later news was received from Pahang that the sultan of Pahang, husband of Raja Ungu, had died. A chief was sent to Pahang to invite Raja Ungu to return to Patani. Raja Ungu returned to Patani bringing with her a daughter she had had with the sultan of Pahang. This daughter was given the name Raja Kuning [Yellow Raja] because her skin was whitish-yellow in color.

During the time that Patani was governed by Raja Biru there was constant rumor that the raja of Siam-Thai was preparing a large armed force to attack Patani. Hearing these rumors, her majesty the raja of Patani was continually worried that they might be true. Her majesty knew that the Siam-Thai people at that time were no longer like the Siam-Thai at the time of the attack on Patani during the reign of her elder sister, Raja Hijau. The power of the Siam-Thai had increased through the purchase of firearms and cannon. On the other hand, within the army of the kingdom of Patani, firearms were not fully utilized. All that was available were those weapons which had been used during the reign of her elder sister, Raja Hijau. In addition, the hope of receiving assistance from foreigners had lessened because most of them had moved away and firearms and cannon were no longer sold in Patani.

In view of these dangers, Her Majesty Raja Biru began to meet with her ministers and chiefs to decide how to obtain firearms in order to protect the independence of Patani and to guard against attack by her enemies. Her majesty proposed the construction of large cannon, as many as possible, as it was understood that the cannon sold by the Europeans were not sufficient to safeguard the independence of Patani and the sovereignty of her rajas.

All of the ministers and chiefs agreed to her majesty's proposal and the manufacture of large cannon began. But because there was not yet a steel foundry in Patani at that time, it was necessary to manufacture the large cannon from brass. In addition, the cannon that were brought by the Europeans to Patani at that time were mainly made from brass. Brass was a type of alloy easily obtainable in Patani at that time.

The manufacture of large cannon proceeded. The craftsman who agreed to make them was a person of Chinese descent who had accepted the Islamic faith, named Tok Kayan. Before embracing Islam he was named Lim Tho Khiam and came from China hoping to make a living in Patani.[48] At that time he was living in the house of a chief of the raja and voluntarily embraced the Islamic faith. Because of his good character he was elevated to become the supervisor of import-export duties at the harbor.[49]

At that time his younger sister also arrived in Patani. Her name was Lim Kun Yew and she came to persuade her elder brother to return. When she learned that her elder brother had adopted Islam and did not want to return, and that he had turned from the religion of his forefathers, with a broken heart she killed herself by hanging from a *janggus (ketirih)* tree.[50] The Chinese of Patani took her corpse and buried it according to the customs of their religion.[51]

This Lim Kun Yew was known as a woman of firm resolve who did not wish to turn her back on the religion of her ancestors and she killed herself because her elder brother had dishonored this religion. All of the Chinese strongly agreed with her, and her death is eternally remembered as a holy sacrifice. They took the janggus tree and made an image of Lim Kun Yew which was then prayed to as a respected holy idol. The Malays of Patani called the statue of Lim Kun Yew Toh Pe Kong Mek and the image has been kept in the Toh Pe Kong in Patani until this very day.[52]

Since there was a craftsman who agreed to cast the large cannon which the female raja of Patani desired, her majesty commanded her chiefs to order anyone in Patani who possessed old brass to present it to her majesty's country to make cannon. It was forbidden to all of the people to send or sell brass outside of the country. For a period of three years anyone who broke this law would suffer the death penalty.

There was a Minangkabau merchant named Saudagar Gembak who came to trade in Patani with a servant named Abdul Mukmin.[53] This merchant had stored large quantities of brass which he wished to sell. In that very year there came a ship from Melaka hoping to purchase brass in Patani. The master of the ship negotiated with Saudagar Gembak hoping to purchase all of his brass. He knew of the prohibition of the raja of Patani, but because the merchant was greedy he agreed to sell the brass and conspired to smuggle the brass at night. When night came, Saudagar Gembak with his servant Abdul Mukmin carried the brass in a sampan to the mouth of the Kuala Ru River towards the Melaka ship which was anchored there.

Unexpectedly the two of them were met by a watchman who arrested them and took them to the harbormaster [*shahbandur*]. When this matter was brought before the raja, her majesty was furious with Saudagar Gembak and his servant. It was ordered that they be killed and their corpses be thrown into the sea at Kuala Ru because of their sin of treachery against the orders of her majesty. The next day the corpses were washed ashore at high tide and they remained there for several days until they became worrisome to the people who came and went there because their odor was so foul. Finally it was necessary to request permission from the raja to bury the corpses. After her majesty assented, the corpses of Saudagar Gembak and his servant were taken to be buried at a place separate from the public cemetery. Their burial place was called "Kubur Tok Panjang," located in present-day Kampung Datu.[54]

After some time much brass was collected by the populace and given to her majesty. The cannon were cast at a place inland from her majesty's citadel and the place where the forge once stood still can be seen to this day near Kampung Kerisik. The soil at that place has become black and not a plant can grow there. The casting of the cannon was an important event in the history of the Malay kingdom of Patani.

After several months the work was completed and three large cannon were made, two of which were very large. Their length was three *depa*, one *hasta*, one *jengkal*, and two and one half fingers, and their projectile was eleven fingers around.[55] The small cannon's length was five hasta and one jengkal, and the span of nine fingers, and its projectile was three fingers in diameter. Her majesty named the two large pieces Sri Negara and Sri Patani, while the small one was named Mahalela. These three cannon were placed on wheeled carts and became the main weapons of war and defense at that time.

Several years thereafter Her Majesty Raja Biru died and her younger sister Raja Ungu, who was the wife of the sultan of Pahang, was elevated to the throne of the kingdom of Patani, replacing her elder sister. Not many years thereafter there came a mission from one of the raja of Johor's sons, who governed the country of Trengganu and who was titled the Yang di Pertuan Muda Johor. His purpose was to propose marriage to the daughter of the raja of Patani. The raja of Patani accepted the engagement [of her daughter] to the Johor raja's son with great gladness. After this the Yang di Pertuan Muda Johor came to Patani with one of his ministers named Incik Idris, together with three thousand of his people and tens of sailing ships, for the wedding. The raja of Patani delayed the marriage for three months in order to complete preparations for the wedding and it became necessary for the Yang di Pertuan Muda Johor to wait in Patani.

While Patani was busy preparing for the royal marriage ceremonies, the raja of Siam-Thai at Ayuthia increased his desire to subjugate Patani as his eternal slave. In the year A.D. 1632 a Siam-Thai naval force led by the commander Okya Decho arrived intending to attack Patani for a second time.[56]

But before the Siam-Thai military force attacked Patani, the Siam-Thai raja established contact with the Dutch Company which was based at Batavia [Jakarta], requesting assistance in his attack. The Dutch Company agreed to send two warships together with weapons to assist the Siam-Thai, but when the Siam-Thai military force arrived at Patani the assistance promised by the Dutch Company had not been sent.

Even so, the Siam-Thai commander was resolved to carry out the attack and proceeded to order his forces to land on Patani's beach. The Patani Malays under the leadership of the raja and her commanders united with all of the people brought by the Yang di Pertuan Muda Johor to resist the attack of the Siam-Thai. The battle was carried out with great ferocity all along the beach. After several days of fighting the Siam-Thai army was still unable to enter the city [bandar] of Patani because of the tremendous resistance of the Patani Malays. In particular, the Patani Malays were well equipped with the weapons of war which

Raja Biru previously had readied. In this battle the three large cannon were used and brought extremely gratifying results because with but a few shots hundreds of Siam-Thai soldiers were killed. The efforts of the Siam-Thai army to enter the city of Patani were completely frustrated.

After several days of fighting, the Siam-Thai commander Okya Decho gave up his hope at defeating the Patani Malays. He saw that the Siam-Thai army was weakened in spirit because of the extremely heavy blows given by the weapons of war of the Patani Malays. He decided to order his forces to return to their ships. As soon as this retreat was completed the Siamese commander ordered his warships to sail back to Siam, humiliatingly disappointed because they had not succeeded in defeating the defenses of the Patani Malays.[57]

When the battle was over, Her Majesty Raja Biru immediately proceeded with the wedding ceremony between her daughter and the Yang di Pertuan Muda Johor. When his marriage was completed the Yang di Pertuan Muda Johor resolved to remain in Patani, not wishing to return to Trengganu.

When the raja of Siam learned that his military commander had not succeeded in subjugating Patani as he had wished, he was extremely angry, which only served to increase his desire to subjugate Patani at all costs. Because of this in the year A.D. 1633 he again sent a mission to Batavia requesting the assistance of the Dutch Company and making known his resolve to attack Patani once again. The Dutch Company agreed to the request of the Siam-Thai raja and undertook to send six warships together with soldiers and their weapons to assist the Siam-Thai. As soon as this agreement was completed the raja of Siam-Thai ordered his military commander Okya Decho to prepare a large military force with the addition of thousands of Siam-Thai soldiers, in full confidence that this time they would be able to breach the defenses of the Patani Malays.

Then the military forces set sail for Patani. When they arrived at Patani the Siamese commander began to land his soldiers on the beach and then assembled to attack the city of Patani. Without hesitation the Patani Malays and the people of the Yang di Pertuan Muda Johor joined together to stop the Siamese attack. All batteries of cannon proceeded to bombard the

Siam-Thai and [the Malays] attacked without pause or retreat. The attack of the Siam-Thai became increasingly strong as they tried with all their might to destroy the defenses of the Patani Malays.

As the battle was fought, the Siam-Thai commander was still awaiting arrival of the assistance promised by the Dutch Company at Batavia. But though he waited and waited, the assistance did not arrive. The Siamese commander was not discouraged, on the contrary he continued fighting and concentrated all of his energy and skill on defeating the defenses of the Patani Malays. The warfare continued for several months until the supply of food brought by the Siam-Thai proved inadequate and the Siam-Thai commander had no means to find food for his people who were fighting. With the appearance of various diseases in his warships, his army began to weaken until the Siam-Thai had no more resources to carry on the battle. Finally the Siam-Thai commander was forced to withdraw his army to the ships and set sail for Singgora, and from there to Ayuthia, bringing home another defeat. Only after the Siam-Thai army had sailed for home did the Dutch warships from Batavia arrive, ready to aid them in attacking Patani according to the agreement between the raja of Siam-Thai and the Dutch Company. But since they arrived too late they did not meet the Siamese army. Upon learning that the Siam-Thai warships had returned they set sail for Batavia.

Two years after the end of the war with the Siamese, in the year A.D. 1635, Her Majesty Raja Ungu died. In a conference at the royal pavilion between the royal family and the chiefs it was agreed to elevate Raja Kuning, the daughter of her majesty, to succeed to the throne of the kingdom of Patani, assisted by her husband the Yang di Pertuan Muda Johor.

In the history of Raja Kuning's life, is it noted that her majesty was a ruler who greatly enjoyed gardening and trading. During the time that her majesty ruled, never did her majesty use the revenue of her kingdom for daily expenditures, although her majesty had the right to that money. Instead, daily expenditures were met by selling of flowers and plants from within her majesty's gardens.

The period of Raja Kuning's reign was the first time that a raja of Patani had directly carried out trade outside of the country.

Her majesty had a trading ship and appointed a captain that she trusted to carry all kinds of trade goods from Patani to all countries. This captain was known as the *Saudagar Raja* [the Raja's Merchant].

Even though the Siamese had attacked Patani three times, and each time their attack had failed with great loss and destruction, nevertheless the intense desire of the raja of Siam to subjugate Patani and the goal of enslaving the Malays never disappeared. With matters thus, he received news of Raja Ungu's death and that the governance of Patani had been entrusted to her daughter, Raja Kuning. Hearing this news, the Siam-Thai Raja sent his commander Okya Decho to Patani with an army. The arrival [of the Siam-Thai army] this time was not aimed at attacking Patani. Rather the visit was a mission from the Siamese raja politely requesting that the raja of Patani submit to placing herself under the suzerainty of the Siam-Thai raja. Raja Kuning did not heed the request of the Siam-Thai raja. On the contrary, it made her heroic blood seethe because such a request showed contempt for her majesty's sovereignty. After the Siamese raja learned that Raja Kuning had not accepted his request, his anger grew and his intense desire to subjugate Patani and enslave the Malays increased in strength. In the year A.D. 1638 the country of Siam-Thai also changed its raja. With this, however, the desire of the kingdom of Siam to subjugate Patani did not disappear.

After the power of the country of Siam-Thai was given to the new raja, the Siam-Thai viceroy who ruled Ligor was ordered to take his people and attack Patani. This viceroy himself was of Japanese descent and was named Yamada. He had come to Siam as a military officer serving the Siam-Thai raja and led a troop of Japanese in the city of Ayuthia. Because of his qualities and service to the Siam-Thai raja, he was elevated to become the Siamese viceroy of Ligor and was given the title Okya Senaphimuk.

When he received the order from the Siam-Thai raja he came with a troop of Japanese and Siam-Ligor soldiers to attack Patani. But the Malays of Patani at that time were quite accustomed to war, greatly treasured the sovereignty of the raja, and knew the advantage of a life of independence. The attack of the Japanese and Siam-Ligor did not succeed this time either.

45

Finally they were forced to return to Ligor, taking their defeat with them.

After four consecutive defeats, the raja of Siam began to understand his weakness, and all parties knew of his intention to subjugate Patani. Even though Patani was only a very small country to the *maharaja* [great raja] of Siam-Thai, the losses which succeeded one another made it evident that it was very difficult to subjugate the Malays, especially as the heroic blood of the Patani Malays at that time was still hot and they were exceedingly loyal to their raja. With such loyalty they were willing to die to the last man in order to defend the sovereignty of her majesty, and the independence of their country.

At that time Patani possessed a very extensive territory with many inhabitants. An Englishman named Hamilton was able to visit Patani at this time and wrote:

> Patani at this time possessed forty-three territories including Trengganu and Kelantan, but when one of the raja of Johor's children came and married, becoming the husband of the female raja of Patani, Trengganu came to be included within the territories under Johor. The sultan of Johor has sent one of his trusted ministers to govern there, leaving only forty-two territories.

He continued: "Patani possesses two river mouths, that is Kuala Patani* and Kuala Bekah.** The city of Patani is called Kota Kedaya."

Continuing, Hamilton wrote:

> The populace of Patani at this time, counting the males (not including females) aged sixteen years to sixty years is 150,000. The inhabitants within the city of Patani

---

*Now called Kuala Ru or Kuala Tok Uguk. The anchorage for all ships and boats which came to trade at Patani was located there.

**Now called Kuala Sungai Patani.

are so numerous that this very large city is filled with a jumble of houses. Beginning at the gate of the royal citadel and continuing to the village there is no gap between the houses. If, for example, a cat were to walk on top of the houses' rafters beginning at the lower end going to the other end it would be possible to proceed without needing to descend to the ground.

Not long thereafter the son of the raja of Johor (husband of Raja Kuning) fell in love with a young women of great beauty, that is one of the "retainers" of the raja in Patani.* Raja Kuning was angry and forced her husband to have made a chastity belt of gold the size of one hasta and the weight of five *kati*.[59] The craftsman who made it was most astonished. When her majesty wore the chastity belt she appeared like a person who was pregnant. This was quite amusing to her chiefs who saw her. But there was none who laughed for fear of her majesty's wrath, and that of her husband.

After Her Majesty Raja Kuning had occupied the throne of the kingdom of Patani for some time the matter of the dispute with her husband became worse. Finally he was forced to depart and return to Johor together with his people.[60] This left Her Majesty Raja Kuning to govern Patani in a condition of peace and security until she passed away.

The date of her majesty's death is not definitely known but it is known that in the year A.D. 1686 a Frenchman visited Patani and noted that at that time Patani still was governed by a female

---

*In the history of Patani it is stated that Raja Kuning kept dancing girls in the palace. One of these was named Dang, who was very clever with love charms. It is said that she kept a talisman [*cemara babi*].[58] Her voice was very gentle and her dancing very good. Because of this, Her Majesty Raja Kuning's husband made her his mistress. This greatly angered Raja Kuning. Her husband took Dang secretly and built a house at a place inland. But finally her majesty's husband came to know of her love charm and stabbed her to death, and her majesty's husband returned to Patani. Because of this behavior there were constant fights between Her Majesty Raja Kuning and her husband.

47

raja. Because of this it is believed that the date of her majesty's death was subsequent to the date of the Frenchman's visit.

Her Majesty Raja Kuning was the very last female raja or Raja Nang Chayang to govern Patani. With her majesty's death there ended the line of succession from Raja Sri Wangsa, the raja who first established the country of Patani. See the genealogy from Raja Sri Wangsa which follows.

Genealogy of Patani's Rajas[a]

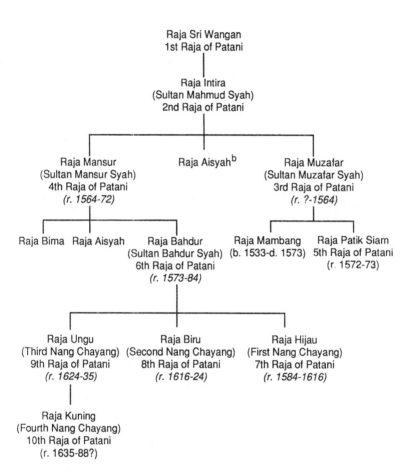

[a] Dates in brackets are from the genealogy of Patani's Rajas found in Teeuw and Wyatt (1970:11)

[b] Raja Aisyah, daughter of Raja Intira, was not included in the author's genealogy.
Because she is mentioned in the text she is included here.

Chapter 3

THE GOVERNMENT OF PATANI IN THE
PERIOD OF DECLINE

When Raja Kuning was dead and there were no more descendants of Raja Sri Wangsa who could be installed as ruler to occupy the throne of the kingdom of Patani, all the royal family and chiefs met to choose a person who was suitable and qualified to ascend the royal throne. An aged chief named Raja Bakar was then living in Kampung Teluk who was deemed most qualified to become the ruler. In this meeting all agreed to elevate Raja Bakar to become ruler and he was invited to ascend the royal throne of Patani. But after Raja Bakar had ruled just a few years on the royal throne, he too died.

Thus the question of choosing a Raja to ascend the throne of the kingdom of Patani was again brought before the council of the royal family and their chiefs. It was decided that those who would be raja of Patani should be descended from a pure raja. At that time in Patani there were none of the line of rajas who could ascend the throne of the kingdom. Therefore, with agreement of the council, one of the sons of the raja of Kelantan, whose name was Raja Mas Kelantan, was invited to become raja of Patani. From that time Patani was ruled by rajas descended from the raja of Kelantan. Raja Mas ruled in Patani a few years until he died and the throne of the kingdom of Patani was given over to his daughter named Raja Mas Chayam.[61]

After a few years Raja Mas Chayam died, also without leaving an heir. Then, with the agreement of the council, a son of a raja named Raja Ahmad from Kampung Dawai (now in the Rakap district) was chosen. He ascended the throne of the kingdom of Patani and was given the title Sultan Mahmud.

While Patani was ruled by Raja Bakar, Raja Mas Kelantan and Raja Mas Chayam, Patani was in a state of peace, never attacked by its enemies, including the Siam-Thai. However, in the question of progress, the country of Patani gradually had begun to decline, particularly in commercial matters. During the rule of the rajas of Patani who were descended from Raja Sri Wangsa, Patani was known as a great commercial center in Southeast Asia and was frequently visited by European peoples. During the rule of the Kelantan rajas commercial progress began to decline. The European peoples all were gone. All that remained in Patani were the Eastern peoples from Japan, China, Indian Muslim businessmen, and Arabs. They lived harmoniously with the Patani Malays, carrying on business peacefully. Because the Indians and Arabs were Muslims, they easily mingled with the Malays and with no obstacle they finally became Malays.

The Siam-Thai, the primary enemies of the people at that time, no longer came to attack Patani because at that time Siam was experiencing such problems as treachery, individual usurpation of power, and frequent civil war, so that the royal throne was constantly being shaken. In addition, the Burmese, who were their constant enemies, did not cease attacking the country of Siam-Thai, with the result that the raja of Siam had no chance to attack and subjugate Patani.

In the year A.D. 1767 the citadel of Ayuthia, center of government of Siam at that time, was captured by the Burmese. Severe disruption was caused when the Burmese entered and ruled Ayuthia. All the minor rajas who ruled the various territories subject to Siam at that time each eagerly desired to rule independently and free themselves from subjugation to the raja of Siam. The raja in the country of Ligor used this opportunity to re-establish his free and independent kingdom. Then he arranged the freedom of his kingdom in southern Siam. The countries of Singgora and Pattalung having become his vassals, he sent his minister to become ruler in these territories.

While Siam was disorganized and its minor rajas in all those territories had established their individual kingdoms, there arose a Siam-Thai chief called Phraya Tak. He was able to assemble a group of Siam-Thai and organize a large army. Then he led this army in a counterattack on the Burmese in Ayuthia. Finally he succeeded and the Burmese were completely routed and killed, and Ayuthia was restored to the hands of the Siam-Thai. The Siam-Thai kingdom was re-established and he himself became its raja. But its center of government was moved to another place in the territory of Thonburi.

Then Phraya Tak, Raja of Siam, sent an army through all his subject territories to defeat the minor rajas who strongly desired independence from the rule of the raja of Siam-Thai. In just a short time all the minor rajas were bowing their heads to him again. Only the raja of Ligor was not yet defeated. Thus in the year A.D. 1769 the Siam-Thai raja launched a great attack on Ligor. Because his strength was greater, the raja of Siam defeated the raja of Ligor. And the raja of Ligor, who had greatly desired independence, was forced to flee to Singgora, but he was pursued by the raja of Siam. Finally the raja of Ligor, the raja of Singgora, and the raja of Pattalung, taking their royal families, fled to Patani and asked for shelter from Sultan Mahmud.

However the Siam-Thai had followed them to the district of Tiba, that is the border of Patani with Siam. From there he sent a mission to Sultan Mahmud asking that the three rajas who had fled from Singgora be arrested and sent to him.

If Sultan Mahmud hesitated to fulfill this wish, he would certainly attack Patani. The mission of the Siam-Thai raja arrived in Patani in the month of December A.D. 1769. Sultan Mahmud met with his chiefs seeking a decision whether or not to accede to the wish of the Siam-Thai raja. Their decision was that it should be acceded to because of concern for the safety and security of the country, which otherwise would be attacked by the Thai raja for such an insignificant reason. In addition, His Majesty Sultan Mahmud felt he had no connection with the raja of Ligor and the other rajas. Afterwards, his majesty ordered his men to arrest the raja of Ligor and take him to the raja of Siam. Then the raja of Siam-Thai sailed back, carrying the three rajas as his prisoners. Since that time Ligor was once again subjugated by the Siam-Thai raja.

The return home of the Siam-Thai raja did not eliminate his evil designs on the country of Patani. He was inflamed with the desire that Patani be subjugated and the Malays there be enslaved, just as he had succeeded in subjugating Ligor, Singgora, and

Pattalung. Because his strength was not yet sufficient, he was forced to be silent, meanwhile awaiting a better time.

With matters thus, in A.D. 1776 the Burmese came to attack the northern part of Siam. The Siam-Thai raja wished to know whether Sultan Mahmud, raja of Patani, feared his influence. As a pretense, he sent a mission to Patani asking Sultan Mahmud to help him to resist the Burmese attack and requesting a sum of 80,000 *baht*.* But Sultan Mahmud did not heed these requests. When the Siam-Thai raja became aware that his wish had not been heeded, he became very angry and his intention to subjugate Patani became increasingly firm.

Meanwhile, in A.D. 1782, the Siam-Thai raja named Phraya Tak or the raja of Thonburi died, murdered by one of his commanders, and this commander was elevated to become raja of Siam-Thai. He was given the title Phraphutta Yotfa Culalok, or Raja Rama the First of the line of Mahachakri. In the reign of this raja the present city of Bangkok was founded.

Two years later, in A.D. 1784, the Burmese came again and attacked Ligor, which was subject to the raja of Siam. The raja of Siam sent his younger brother, who was the raja muda, with an army to fight the Burmese. This army went forth from Bangkok with several warships toward Ligor. When they arrived at Ligor the Siam-Thai commander immediately landed his troops and united with the force of Siam-Ligor to fight the Burmese. The war continued for several months, after which the Burmese were forced to retreat home having been defeated by the Siam-Thai force from Bangkok.

After the end of the war, the raja muda of Siam took his army to Singgora in order to put in order affairs of government there. Having finished his work, he sent a mission to Patani asking Sultan Mahmud to submit to him properly. When the mission of the Siam-Thai raja arrived in Patani, Sultan Mahmud called a meeting of his chiefs. It was unanimously decided to reject the demand to submit, which was aimed at usurping the sovereignty of the raja and the freedom of the country of Patani.

---

*Similar missions also were sent to the sultans of Kelantan and Trengganu as well as Patani.

This decision was announced to the Thai mission. When the Thai raja knew that his desire was unfilled and that in addition he had received a proud answer from Sultan Mahmud, the breath of imperialism flared hotly in his heart and he decided to attack Patani. Then he told his commander named Phraya Kalahom to take his army and attack Patani and he ordered the commander to fight to the end until Patani became subjugated.[62]

Sultan Mahmud, after the departure of the Siam-Thai mission, was certain that this time the Siam-Thai would attack Patani. Therefore his majesty, with no further delay, ordered weapons of war to be assembled, defense forts to be built, and as many war supplies as could be obtained be prepared.

But unhappily the position of Patani at that time was weak, its power had declined, and all its weapons of war would be insufficient if the war were long. Since the end of war with the Siam-Thai during the reign of Raja Kuning, almost half a century earlier, Patani had not equipped itself with weapons of war as no enemies had come to attack. During that time the Patani Malays had lived securely and peacefully and they had forgotten how to prepare for war. Tactics for guarding their land were nearly forgotten. Thus as time passed the bravery of the Malays had gradually weakened while the weapons which were kept in the armories were nearly useless and not of the same standard as the new weapons in the hands of the Thai army.

Thus was the situation. Nevertheless, seeing the attitude of the Siam-Thai raja, who fully intended to subjugate Patani, Sultan Mahmud did not lose hope. Rather, his majesty immediately assembled the old weapons which still existed and advised his people that the coming war would determine the success or failure and the life or death of the Malay kingdom of Patani, asking his people to unite and take full part in the fight to defend the independence of their people and kingdom. Sultan Mahmud's request was gladly received by the people of Patani and all were willing to resist the wickedness of the Siam-Thai even though they were forced to sacrifice themselves and break their limbs and bodies. It was better to sacrifice themselves thus in war to defend their independence than to live as vassals dominated by the Siam-Thai.

53

When the Siamese army approached Patani, all the people of Patani were mobilized by Sultan Mahmud to assemble outside the royal citadel and were divided into two forces. The first force was ordered to guard the forts on the shore in order to defend against landings by the Siam-Thai from their warships. The second force was ordered to guard the front of the royal citadel. All weapons, including cannon and cannonballs, were divided equally. The large cannon Sri Negara and Sri Patani which had once before defeated the Thai were again brought out and placed outside the citadel to await the official order to let fly their reliable projectiles.

Both defense forces awaited the moment to repulse the Siam-Thai attack. Not many days later the Thai army led by Phraya Kalahom arrived in Kuala Patani and anchored there while awaiting a propitious time to launch its attack. At this most important moment, in the group of Sultan Mahmud's chiefs there was a Siam-Thai named Nai Chanthong who came originally from Siam-Ligor to live in Patani with some followers. He had been of great service to the kingdom of Patani so that Sultan Mahmud placed full confidence in him and had appointed him a royal chief.

While the Siam-Thai army was anchored in Kuala Patani, there rose in him an evil feeling toward the kingdom of Patani, and wishing to show devotion to his race and kingdom, he devised an evil plan. Quickly he went before His Majesty Sultan Mahmud to say that he was willing to fight the Siam-Thai invasion but he wished to be appointed the leader of the force of Malays defending the forts on the beach, and he requested the sultan give him a large boat five cubits long to be equipped with cannon and weapons. Trustingly, Sultan Mahmud granted his request and Nai Chanthong with his boat pretended to set off for the defense forts on the shore. Here he began to put his evil plan into effect against the Patani kingdom.

When midnight came, when the world is dark and gloomy and shelters a person who would do evil, Nai Chanthong went out in his boat toward the Siam-Thai warships and asked to meet with commander Phraya Kalahom. Upon meeting him, he [Nai Chanthong] revealed the secrets of the Patani Malays' defenses. Phraya Kalahom was very pleased to learn the secrets of the Malay defenses. He was sure that this time his army would certainly win and that this time it was assured that the kingdom of Patani would topple, overturned by his army.

When the proper moment arrived, the commander began to direct his cannon to bombard the Malay defense forts on the beach and quickly he landed his troops on the beach under cover of the projectiles fired by his cannon. Unfortunately every time a shell was fired by the Thai cannon it fell in a Malay fort, so that after just a few rounds many Malays were killed. However the Malays determinedly and fiercely returned the fire. The attack and bombardment of the Siam-Thai increased in intensity until all the Thai forces had come up on the beach and with all their combined strength attacked the Malay forts. Suddenly the Malay position was surrounded and they were cut off from the second force which was defending the citadel. Although they were surrounded and their hope was gone, the Malays in the forts continued to resist without faltering. Afterwards the defense of the Malays on the shore was destroyed and the forts and their cannon were captured by the Siam-Thai.

After the defensive line of the Malays on the shore fell, commander Phraya Kalahom reassembled his remaining military power and immediately launched his attack on the citadel. The commander's attack met fierce opposition from the Malay defenders in front of the royal citadel, and Sultan Mahmud himself came forth to organize the defense. The cannon Sri Negara and Sri Patani too began to fire their trusty projectiles hitting the Siam-Thai advance and fierce hand-to-hand fighting with swords and daggers ensued.

This battle continued for several days without ceasing. Sadly, Sultan Mahmud was struck by a cannonball fired by the Siam-Thai, and his majesty fell and died in the midst of the battle. Not many hours after the death of his majesty, the defenses of the Malays in front of the royal citadel were pierced and the Siam-Thai attack continued just as powerfully. The Malay defense reached its final moment and broke, and everyone scattered. The royal citadel fell into the hands of the Siam-Thai and the battle ended with the defeat of the Malays.

This defeat was the first in the history of the Malay kingdom of Patani, and signified the loss of independence of the Malay kingdom of Patani and the abolition of the sovereignty of the

Malay rajas which had been defended for hundreds of years. The purpose of the Siam-Thai raja was accomplished, which he had long desired, to subjugate Patani and to enslave its people.

The loss of the Patani Malays on this occasion was caused by several factors, the most important of which were:

(1) The secrets of the Malay defense and their strength were revealed by Nai Chanthong to the Siam-Thai commander;
(2) Sultan Mahmud died in the battle;
(3) The supply of weapons of the Malays was insufficient;
(4) The military might of the Siam-Thai was greater than the Malays.

All the Patani Malay defenses were destroyed, and Patani fell under the yoke of Thai subjugation. This was the first defeat of the country of Patani, which had been sovereign and independent for hundreds of years since the reign of the Raja Sri Wangsa, so the defeat was very significant in the history of the Malay kingdom of Patani. Thus the struggle and sacrifice of the Patani rajas for hundreds of years to defend their royal sovereignty and the independence of the Malays finally had achieved a most saddening result. The sovereignty of the Patani rajas and the independence of the Malays fell under the yoke of Thai subjugation, and this defeat brought Patani directly under the Siam-Thai yoke to this day.

After capturing all the defenses of the Malays, the first thing the Thai in Patani did was to arrest and kill unarmed Patani Malay men, women, and young children, and to steal all property and weapons. Then the palace of the late Sultan Mahmud was burnt to the ground.

For about a month the Siam-Thai sacked Patani in order to gain complete revenge on the Patani Malays, who had been characterized as their greatest enemy. The commander Phraya Kalahom began to organize the laws of government in Patani according to the pattern of laws of subjugation and took away the sovereignty of the raja and his chiefs.

After establishing these laws, the Siamese commander ordered his troops to return to the warships, weigh anchor, and sail back to Bangkok, carrying some Malay captives, including men, women, and children, along with the booty of war. Among this booty, the most valuable thing to the Malays were the great cannon made in the reign of Raja Biru. One of them was carried along with the captives to Bangkok, but the second fell into the sea off Kuala Patani while the Siam-Thai were carrying it up to the ship. One was taken to Bangkok. To this day the great Patani cannon decorates the front of the office of the Minister of War in Bangkok.

The laws of government composed by the Thai commander before his return to Bangkok included the appointment of a Malay to be ruler of Patani as a puppet raja. The administration of the country was put under the supervision of the Siam-Thai raja in Ligor, and he was forced to send tribute to Bangkok to show his loyalty.[*] The puppet raja appointed by the Siam-Thai was Raja Bendang Badang named Tungku Lamidin.[65]

When Tungku Lamidin was elevated by Siam to be the raja of Patani, his first duty was to rebuild the palace and reassemble the people of Patani, who had fled. But when he saw the palace in Kerisik was completely destroyed and deserted because many of the people had died in the war and many more had been captured by Siam and taken to Bangkok, Tungku Lamidin did not want to stay in Kerisik. Then his majesty built a new palace in Perawan and appointed a chief named Datuk Pangkalan, who lived in Kampung Pangkalan Besar, to be ruler in Kerisik.[66]

Although Tungku Lamidin had been appointed by the Siam-Thai to be a puppet raja, a feeling of sadness took root in his heart in account of the deeds of the Siam-Thai against the Patani Malays. Therefore his majesty firmly resolved to seek revenge for

----

[*]What tribute was sent by the raja of Patani to the raja of Siam at that time is not yet clearly known. In later times tribute was known to be sent once every three years in the form of a flowering tree with five tiers of leaves [commonly known as the *bunga emas*], all made of ten karat gold.[63] Besides this golden flowering tree, it also was necessary to send with it three golden boxes and three lances also plated with gold. The total gold making up the flowing tree, boxes and lances was no less than forty *tahil* in weight.[64]

this defeat and to free the kingdom of Patani from the yoke of Siam-Thai subjugation. His majesty only awaited a good opportunity to carry out this intention.

With matters thus, in A.D. 1789 his majesty sent a mission carrying a letter to the raja of Annam (Vietnam) in Indochina, named Raja "Wan Cheng Su," inviting that raja to join him in attacking Siam. His majesty would attack southern Siam and the raja of Annam would attack from the north.

Unfortunately the raja of Annam sent Tungku Lamidin's letter to the raja of Siam in Bangkok. When the raja of Siam learned of the raja of Patani's plan he became very angry and ordered his commander Phraya Kelahom to arrest the raja of Patani. Meanwhile Tungku Lamidin had completely re-equipped his army and he rose up with his troops and attacked the country of Tiba, driving out the Siam-Thai there. Immediately thereafter he invaded the territory of Chenak, meeting little opposition and finally arriving at Singgora. When his majesty arrived at Singgora he met a force of Siam-Thai who were fortified at Kampung Bukit Anak Gajah. There they fought for several days.

News of the Malay attack on Singgora reached the Siam-Thai raja in Ligor, who sent reinforcements to help the Singgora Siam-Thai. The attack of the Malays under the direction of Tungku Lamidin became increasingly ferocious, and finally the defense of the Singgora Siam-Thai was defeated. The Siam-Thai rajas of Singgora and Ligor fled to the country of Pattalung, but they were immediately pursued by the Malays so that a battle also took place in the country of Pattalung.

With matters thus, the force of commander Phraya Kalahom arrived from Bangkok seeking to capture the raja of Patani. This army united with the rajas of Singgora and Ligor and together they fought against the Patani attack. This war continued fiercely for three years with no winner or loser. Because the war lasted so long, the Malay forces became weakened. Far from their home base, it was very difficult for them to get assistance of food and weapons from Patani. In the end Tungku Lamidin was forced to withdraw his people to Patani.

The retreat of Tungku Lamidin did not bring any benefit whatsoever to his majesty as it provided an opportunity for the Siamese to launch their counterattack. All during their retreat they were constantly followed by the Siam-Thai. Finally the Malays arrived in Patani and together they prepared to defend Perawan and awaited the Siamese attack.

Because the Siamese army was collected from three large forces they were more numerous than the Malays. In the end Perawan was surrounded by the Siamese and they cut all communication of the Malays with their comrades outside the citadel. With matters thus, after a long Malay defense Perawan finally fell into the hands of the Siamese and Tungku Lamidin was arrested by the Siamese. His majesty was sentenced to be killed for his crime of treachery against the Siam-Thai Raja in Bangkok. Then the Malays broke and fled. This defeat occurred in 1791, the second defeat in the history of the Malay kingdom of Patani. As usual the Siam-Thai entered Perawan capturing and killing Malays and stealing all their property. When they were sated with terrorizing, they returned to Singgora, taking some Malay captives.

Before the Thais returned, they chose a Malay chief to be elevated as raja to rule Patani, "Datuk Pangkalan," who they gave the title Luang.[67] Because of this all children of this chief also are called Luang. In order to watch over the Malays and guard against treachery they also appointed a Siamese chief named "Laksamana Dajang"[68] to control the Malay chiefs and a few Siam-Thai were also asked to remain to keep order in Patani.

Afterwards affairs in Patani were somewhat calmer but the ruler, Datuk Pangkalan, frequently quarreled with the Siamese because he had no freedom to conduct the government of the country. He was continually surrounded by Siam-Thai whose attitude was evil and who continually committed cruelties against the Patani Malay people. Therefore in A.D. 1808 there arose a fierce dispute between Datuk Pangkalan and the Siamese.

Losing his patience, Datuk Pangkalan came with his men and launched a surprise attack against the Siam-Thai. They were forced to save themselves and flee with their leader Laksamana Dajang to Singgora. The raja of Singgora sent a letter to Bangkok stating that Datuk Pangkalan and the Patani Malays were traitors to the Siam-Thai raja. Meanwhile, the raja of Ligor and the raja of Singgora came with their troops to Patani in order to arrest Datuk Pangkalan.

In Patani all the families of the chiefs, that is Datuk Pangkalan, Datuk Sai, Datuk Pujud, and others, were ready and collected their strength, awaiting the arrival of the Siamese from Ligor and Singgora. When the Siamese arrived they fought the people of Patani for months. The people of Patani under the leadership of the chiefs fought to the end, firmly determined to drive the Siamese from Patani and free themselves from the yoke of Thai subjugation. Against this holy purpose, the Siamese were lost and retreated to Singgora, and Laksamana Dajang returned to Ligor.

A few months later, a Thai force from Bangkok led by Phraya Kalahom arrived with several warships and landed, followed by Siamese from Singgora and Ligor. This time the battle took place simultaneously on land and sea, the land battle occurring in Bawarah, and the sea battle at Kerisik. Finally the Patani Malays lost. Datuk Pangkalan died in the struggle, and all the other chiefs fled.

After achieving victory, the exulting Siam-Thai entered and ruled Patani, took Malays prisoner, seized all their possessions, and arranged the laws of the government in Patani to suit their wishes. Then the Siam-Thai began to carry out their plan to destroy the sovereignty of the Malay rajas. They elevated a Siam-Thai named "Nai Khwan Sai" to be raja of Patani. After completing the organization of the government of Patani, commander Phraya Kalahom returned to Bangkok with his army. Nai Khwan Sai was a son of the raja of Chenak, who was descended from a Chinese who came to do business in Chenak. Afterwards Nai Khwan Sai came to rule in Patani and brought several hundred Singgora Siamese and [they] made their settlement in the city.

Thenceforth, the sovereignty of the Malay rajas and the country of Patani was eliminated and full power fell into the hands of the Siam-Thai. In the next few years Raja Khwan Sai died and was succeeded by his son "Nai Phai" who became raja of Patani. A son of his older brother named "Nai Yim Sai" was given the title Luang Sawatphakdi and elevated to become his aide.

During the time Nai Phai ruled the country of Patani as raja, the situation in the country was not as peaceful as in the reign of the previous Malay rajas. Because the Siamese considered themselves more powerful, they continually acted cruelly and fiercely toward the Malays of Patani, and were always in conflict with the Malays. This state of affairs caused the Malays to hate them deeply.

Nai Phai was of the opinion that the Malays were always plotting revenge against the Siamese, and he became worried that the Malays might revolt and demand their freedom. Therefore he sent a letter to the raja of Singgora expressing his concern, and the raja of Singgora conveyed this concern to the raja of Siam in Bangkok. The question was brought before a meeting with his ministers to decide on consolidating their rule in the subject territory of Patani.

The conference agreed that the strength of Patani should be dispersed so that it could be ruled more easily. In this way the position of the Malays could be weakened. The raja of Siam sent one of his ministers named "Phraya Aphaisongkhram" to Singgora to confer with the raja of Singgora in order to divide the country of Patani into seven small provinces, Patani, Jering, Nongchik, Yala, Sia, Rahman, and Ligeh.

Thus the country of Patani which before was ruled by just one raja and never divided, now had been split up into several provinces. It was split up by the raja of Siam with the intention of weakening the strength of the Malays in order to make it easy for him to rule and enslave the Malays according to the principles of colonization (imperialism), that is, "divide and rule." When the task of dividing Patani was complete, Nai Phai was elevated to become raja of Jering and to him was surrendered the authority to supervise all the other provinces. All matters of internal government were placed beneath the care and control of the raja of Singgora. For each of those provinces Nai Phai was allowed to choose men who he trusted and he sent them to rule in each of those provinces and gave them the rank of raja.

The men chosen by Nai Phai and sent to govern in the provinces are as follows:

(1) Tuan Sulong was elevated to be the raja of Patani and resided in Kota Kerisik;

(2) Tuan Nik was elevated to be the raja of Nongchik and resided in Kota Nongchik;[69]

(3) Tuan Mansor was elevated to become the raja of Rahman and resided in Kota Baharu;

(4) Tuan Jalur was elevated to be the raja of Yala and resided in Yala;

(5) Nik Dah was elevated to be the raja of Ligeh and resided in Kota Ligeh;

(6) Nik Dih was elevated to be the raja of Sia and resided in Jeringu.

Tuan Sulong, who became the raja of Patani, was a grandchild of Datuk Pangkalan and resided with his family in Kampung Kerisik. Nai Phai trusted all the men completely except for him. While Tuan Sulong was raja of Patani, his majesty strongly stressed Islamic religious affairs and it was his majesty who constructed the mosque in Pintu Gerbang, and remains of which still can be found in Kampung Kerisik today.

In A.D. 1817 Tuan Jalur who ruled the province of Yala died and was succeeded by his son Tuan Bangkok. Then Tuan Nik, raja of Nongchik, also died and Tuan Kechil, younger brother of Tuan Sulong, the raja of Patani, was elevated to succeed him and rule in Nongchik. A few years later Tuan Mansur, raja of Rahman, also died and was succeeded by his son named Tuan Kundur. Thus was the government in Patani while it was dominated by the authority of the Siamese. The system of government was under the yoke of their colonization.

Beginning at this point the country of Patani was involved with the country of Kedah. Therefore it is best if we introduce some of Kedah's history while it was connected with the history of the kingdom of Patani and the Thai so that we may easily understand it. At that time the country of Kedah was ruled by a Malay raja known as Sultan Ahmad Tajud'din Abdulhalim Shah or Tungku Pengeran. His majesty was defeated by the Siam-Thai raja and fled to save himself in Melaka. The country of Kedah came to be ruled by a son of the raja of Siam-Ligor.

In A.D. 1831 a son from the royal family of Kedah together with Tungku Rudin assembled all the people of Kedah who were still loyal to their raja and launched an attack on the Siamese in Kedah. Finally they regained the royal palace occupied by the Siamese raja and the Siamese raja with his chiefs fled back to

Singgora. There he conferred with the raja of Singgora and his father the raja of Ligor in order to form a large force to reconquer the people of Kedah. Each agreed to this plan and they gathered an armed force of the combined men of Singgora and Siam-Ligor.

This Siamese force launched a heavy counterattack on Kedah. Tungku Din himself went out to lead the people of Kedah in fighting the Siam-Thai attack. This battle continued, but the Siamese attack did not succeed in conquering the people of Kedah, and the Siamese Raja was forced to retreat with his army to Singgora. Throughout his retreat he was pursued and attacked by Tungku Din and his people as far as Singgora.

Seeing that the attack of the Kedah people had reached his country, the raja of Singgora informed the raja of Siam in Bangkok and asked him for help quickly. A letter was also sent to Raja Nai Phai in Patani asking that help be sent to him to fight the Kedah people.

When the letter arrived in Patani, Raja Nai Phai directed all the rajas of the six provinces in Patani to bring their people and assemble in the district of Jering (Jambu) because they were to be sent to the raja of Singgora. The raja of Patani, the raja of Nongchik, the raja of Ligeh, and the raja of Yala each brought their people to assemble in Jering. Only the raja of Sia and the raja of Rahman did not come. Nai Phai asked those rajas to take their men and go to Singgora, but the rajas were reluctant to follow his order because they knew their men would be taken to fight their brothers, the people of Kedah, who were the same type of people [that is, Malays] as they. Nai Phai was forced to carry out harsh measures and threats until the four rajas were willing to take their men to Singgora. Only then did his harsh measures cease.

With matters thus, the four rajas secretly met to discuss their problem. Each was firmly opposed to taking their men to Singgora to fight their brothers the people of Kedah and each agreed to rebel against the Raja Nai Phai and the Siamese who were in Patani.

The four rajas ordered their men to take up their weapons and unite in attacking the Siamese in Patani. Because the Siamese were very few in number they were incapable of fighting the Malay revolt. Many Siamese were killed and many were able to flee to

Singgora. But they were pursued by the Malays as far as Tiba and Chenak. When they crossed the border of Singgora, the Malays met their brothers, the people of Kedah, who were then fighting the Siamese of Singgora.

The Malays of Patani united with their Kedah brothers and together fought the Siam-Thai. In this battle the Malays of Patani fortified themselves at Bukit Anak Gajah and Kampung Bangkadan. While the battle was fiercely raging, a force of Siam-Thai from Bangkok arrived led by Phraya Phraklang who had been sent by their raja to help the raja of Singgora.[70] This was a large military force, well-equipped with many weapons. After he had united with the Singgora Siamese, their strength to fight the Malays increased. But the Malays continued to fight without considering the greater power of their enemies. With matters thus, Tungku Kudin, commander of the Kedah men, died in the fighting and the people of Kedah scattered and fled. The Malays of Patani saw their brothers were scattered, and realizing they did not have the means to fight the more powerful Thai, they were forced to retreat to Patani, where they determined to make their final stand.

The Siam-Thai commander Phraya Phraklang assembled all the Siamese forces and divided them into two troops. The first was sent to attack the Kedah people and the second force was sent to attack the people of Patani. The first troop launched their attack on Kedah, concentrating all their strength. After Kedah was again subjugated, the Siamese raja who had ruled previously was again elevated to be the Siamese ruler. After the conclusion of their battle with the people of Kedah, the second force went forth, led by Phraya Phraklang himself, toward Patani with several of his warships. When they arrived in Patani he landed his men on the beach at Kuala Patani and invaded the country. The Malays under the leadership of their four rajas put up a stout defense.

Tuan Sulong, who was ruler of Patani at that time, was a nephew of Long Ahmad, the sultan of Kelantan. When he learned that Patani was attacked by the Siamese, His Majesty Long Ahmad sent a troop of Kelantan people to help the people of Patani, who were at war with the Siam-Thai. This troop was led by the raja muda of Kampung Laut, his son Tungku Besar (Tungku Ahmad), and the raja of Banggul. Furthermore, the sultan of Trengganu sent a force to aid Patani led by Panglima Tungku Indris, Panglima Incik Kilan, Panglima Wan Kamal, and Panglima Incik Ismail.[71] After these reinforcements arrived in Patani, they joined the people of Patani to battle the Siamese.

This battle proceeded with the greatest ferocity in the history of Patani. Phraya Phraklang ordered the Siamese to fight to the finish and he did not care that the losses and destruction he sustained were greater than that of the Malays. Finally the Malay defenses collapsed and the gate of victory was opened to the Siamese. The Malays, who were not powerful enough to resist their attack, were forced to scatter. The people of Kelantan and Trengganu with their chiefs retreated to their countries.

Tuan Sulong, raja of Patani, and Tuan Kundur, raja of Yala, fled with their wives and children to sanctuary in Kelantan. At the same time Tuan Kechil, raja of Nongchik, and Nik Dah, raja of Ligeh, fled to the interior of Patani, but they were pursued by the Siamese as far as the district of Jarum on the Perak border and there occurred a battle between the two Rajas and the Siamese. Tuan Kechil died in the battle and Nik Dah escaped to Perak. After the Rajas of Patani had all fled, the people of Patani suffered sorrowfully from oppression, murder, and rape by the Siam-Thai who prided themselves on their victories. All the property and foodstuffs of the Malays, such as rice, fowl, and others, were completely loaded aboard the ships as booty.

When they were sated with sacking Patani, Phraya Phraklang, the Siamese commander, began to equip his army to invade Kelantan and Trengganu, wishing to gain revenge for the actions of their rajas, who had aided the Malays of Patani in battling the Siamese.

When this became known to Long Mahmud, sultan of Kelantan, his majesty worried lest Kelantan be attacked and subjugated by the Siam-Thai. In order to ensure that Kelantan not suffer the same fate as Patani, the sultan of Kelantan sent a peace mission to Phraya Phraklang seeking to submit to the raja of Siam and to pay for his mistake with a sum of $50,000. Tuan Sulong, raja of Patani, and Tuan Kundur, raja of Yala, and their wives and children who were in Kelantan, were sent back to the

Siamese commander. With this, the plan to attack Kelantan was set aside.

Then the Siam-Thai commander sent a mission to the sultan of Trengganu, reminding him of his mistake in aiding the people of Patani, and forcing him to send back all the people of Patani who had come for sanctuary in Trengganu, especially the Patani commanders Panglima Damit, Panglima Mahmud, Panglima Pia, and Panglima Ahmad. All the people of Patani and their commanders were surrendered by the sultan of Trengganu to the Siamese commander, who was waiting in Patani.

After the government in Patani was re-established by the Siamese commander, in the month of September 1832 the Siam-Thai army returned to Bangkok, carrying with them prisoners of war and possessions seized in Patani. The Patani Malay captives taken by Siam this time were no less than 4,000 people, men, women, and children. The suffering borne by the Malays who were confined in the Siam-Thai warships during the journey to Bangkok cannot be written and some of them died in the ships before arriving in Bangkok.[72]

Before the Siamese returned, their commander chose successors to those rajas of the small provinces of Patani who had been caught or who had died:

(1) In Patani, Nik Yusuf of Gerisik was chosen;
(2) In Nongchik, Nai Min, a Siamese of Chenak, was chosen;
(3) In Yala, Nai Yim Sai (Luang Sawatphakdi), aide of Raja Nai Phai, was chosen;
(4) In Ligeh, Nik Bungsu of Bapu, who was faithful to Nai Phai, was chosen.

Nai Yim Sai, raja of Yala, resided in Kubang Teras. Nik Bongsu, raja of Ligeh, resided in Tanjong Emas. Nik Yusuf, raja of Patani, resided in Kuala Bekah, downriver from present-day Gedung China.

After that time the countries of Patani and Kedah were under the authority of the raja of Siam. Kedah was ruled by a son of the Siamese raja of Ligor and Patani was ruled by rajas appointed by the Siam-Thai. Their rule continued until the year

A.D. 1838. There were two princes in the family of the raja of Kedah named Tungku Mahmud Sa'ad and Tungku Abdullah. These two princes devised a secret plan of action to overturn the power of the Siamese raja and retake control of the Malay kingdom of Kedah. When the appointed day and hour arrived, the people of Kedah under the leadership of the two princes attacked the Siamese, and immediately retook the palace and killed the Siamese in Kedah, but their raja was able to flee to Singgora with his people.

The fleeing Siamese were immediately followed the pursued by the people of Kedah as far as Chenak, and here the Singgora Siamese came to aid their comrades in resisting the attack of the Kedah people. Because the Kedah people's attack became fiercer and fiercer, the raja of Singgora sent a messenger to Bangkok to ask for immediate aid. A similar message was sent to Raja Nai Phai in Jering.

Raja Nai Phai called all the rajas of these provinces to bring their people to Singgora. Because these rajas were loyal to Raja Nai Phai and had for long been tools of his rule, they did not pose any obstacle to Raja Nai Phai and brought their people to Singgora. But when they arrived in Chenak, many of the people of Patani ran from their rajas because they did not want to help the Siamese. They were to be taken to fight their brothers, the people of Kedah. The people of Patani went to join their brothers the people of Kedah and turned to fight the Siamese.

This battle continued for some time until the Malays were weak. Tungku Mahmud Sa'ad, leader of the people of Kedah, died in the fight and Tungku Abdullah retreated with his people to Kedah. His retreat was followed by Siamese attacks on his rear as far as Kedah. Because the Kedah peoples' strength had been exhausted in the battle, Kedah easily fell again into the hands of the Siamese, and the Patani Malays who had joined the Kedah people were forced to flee.

After the end of the battle, the raja of Singgora asked the rajas of Patani from the six provinces to return with their subjects because he worried that a revolt of the Patani Malays might arise. Not many years later Raja Nai Phai, who ruled in the province of Jering, died. The center of government in Singgora was informed of his death. By order of the raja of Singgora, Nai Yim Sai, raja at Yala, was appointed to be the raja ruling in Jering. Then he appointed a Singgora Siamese named Nai Muang to be raja ruling in Yala, and Nai Muang moved from Kota Kubang and established a new town of Kampung Seting, across the Sungai Besar.

In A.D. 1842 Kelantan was ruled by Sultan Tuan Senik the Red Mouth.[73] In this year an atmosphere of conflict clouded the family of the raja of Kelantan. This conflict occurred between the sultan and several members of his family, including Sultan Dewa (Raja Penembang), the raja muda, Tungku Sri Indra, and Tungku Mahmud (Tungku Besar), son of the raja muda of Kampung Laut. This dispute caused enmity and civil war between the sultan and the rajas mentioned.

After the civil war had continued for some time and there was no hope of obtaining peace, the two sides submitted the matter to the raja of Siam in Bangkok. This submission was well received by the raja of Siam. He sent one of his chiefs named Phraya Chaiya Thainam with the raja of Ligor and the raja of Singgora to Kelantan as intermediaries to stop the fighting.

At the same time that the Thai rajas were working to end the civil war in Kelantan, Nai Yi Sai (Luang Sawatphakdi), raja of Jering, died. Nik Yusuf, raja of Patani, was elevated to succeed him, and because Patani had no raja, Tungku Mahmud (Tungku Besar) son of the raja muda of Kampung Laut was invited to move to Patani and he was officially installed as raja to rule Patani. All internal administration was put under the control and care of the Siamese raja of Singgora. Sultan Dewa went to Ligor and remained there permanently.

In this transfer to Patani, Tungku Mahmud was accompanied by his relatives, including Tungku Tuan Menanjiwa and Tungku Banggul, together with their families, and also by Tungku Long Ahmad, raja of Bukit. All these rajas stayed together with Tungku Mahmud in Patani. At first Tungku Mahmud established his palace compound across from the end of the Peninsula, now called Kampung Tungku Besar Semarak, but not long afterward he decided that the area of that compound was not suitable. He and his relatives then moved and established a new palace in Kampung "Chabang Tiga" and to this day this is the site of the palace of the rajas of Patani.

After Tungku Mahmud was chosen to become the raja of Patani, he was given the title Sultan Mahmud, but by the raja of Siam in Bangkok he was titled Phraya Tani. At the wish and order of the raja of Siam, all the royal family who accompanied Tungku Mahmud to Patani were given their own positions. The raja of Banggul was chosen to become Phraya Phitak, which means the office of adviser to the sultan of Patani, and all the other rajas also were chosen to become high officers of the kingdom. After two years the raja of Banggul and Tungku Long Ahmad, the raja of Bukit, both died in Patani. Then Tungku Tengah, son of the raja of Banggul, who chosen to become Phraya Phitak to replace his father.

Since that time, the country of Patani began to be ruled by rajas from Kelantan who were appointed by the raja of Siam. Internal government was carried out under the supervision and control of the raja of Siam, through the administrative center at Singgora. Thus the sovereignty of Sultan Mahmud and his chiefs went no further than the end of the index finger of the raja of Siam. In other words, the government operated according to the beckoning of the finger of the raja of Siam, whose wishes were based on principles of their subjugation. Only in the era of the rule of Sultan Mahmud did the atmosphere in Patani gradually become increasingly calm and peaceful.

Not long afterward, Nai Min, raja of the province of Nongchik was removed from office by the raja of Siam because he governed ineffectively. Nai Kliang, son to Nai Yi Sai, formerly the raja of Jering, was appointed raja of Nongchik. Nai Kliang moved his center of government from Nongchik to Kampung Tok Jong. Afterward, Nai Muang, raja of Yala, also was dismissed from his office by the raja of Siam because he was unqualified to rule. Tungku Mahmud Salih (Tuan Batu Putih) was appointed to become raja of Yala and Tungku Mahmud Salih moved the center of his government to Kampung Yala, where it had been in earlier times.

Then Nik Dah, raja of the province of Sia and who lived in Jering, died; Tungku Halal Aladin (Nik Lebai), his son, was appointed to become the raja there.[74] In the year A.D. 1853 Nik Yusuf, raja of the province of Jering, also died. This raja was called Raja Tok Ki by the people of Patani.[75] The raja of Siam at

Singgora chose Sultan Dewa who lived in Ligor to become raja in the province of Jering to replace him. After that Sultan Dewa moved with his children to rule in Jering and his son Tungku Sulong was elevated to become his aide with the title Luang Sunthonraya.

After Sultan Dewa had been raja ruling in Jering for approximately one year he too died and his son Tungku Sulong requested permission from the raja of Siam to move back to Kelantan because he did not want to stay in Jering any more. Nik Timung, son of raja Nik Yusuf, former raja of Jering, was then appointed to become raja ruling in Jering.

In the year A.D. 1856 Sultan Mahmud, raja of Patani, also died. His majesty was buried in the cemetery of Tanjung Datuk, therefore he is referred to as Almarhum Tanjung to this day. At his death, his majesty left four sons and two daughters, namely:

(1) Tungku Putih, who later became the second Raja of Patani;
(2) Tungku Bulat (Tungku Haji Tua);
(3) Tungku Hassan (Tungku Nik Mandarahan);
(4) Tungku Bongsu (Tungku Sulaiman Sharit Aladin, fourth Raja of Patani);[76]
(5) Tungku Temenal, married to Raja Rahman;
(6) Tungku Laboh, married to Tungku Chik, son of Tungku Banggul.

With the agreement of the raja at Siam, Tungku Putih was appointed to become raja of Patani in place of his father and given the title "Phraya Wichitphakdi."*

---

*In the reign of Tungku Putih the titles in the Siamese language for the raja of Patani and his chief men were officially fixed, as follows: the title for the raja of Patani was Phraya Wichitphakdi; the title for the adviser of the raja was Phraya Phithakthammasunthon; the title of the heir apparent was Phraya Si Burirattaphanit; the title of his assistant was Phraya Phiphitphakdi. From then on these titles were given by the raja of Siam to anyone who occupied these offices.[77]

In the reign of Tungku Putih the country of Patani became increasingly populous and many foreign businessmen came to do business in Patani. Among them the most numerous were the Chinese. Because of the large number of these people the village in which they lived became known as Kampung China, as it is today.

Not many years later Tuan Kundur, raja at Rahman, and Tungku Mahmud Salih (Tuan Batu Putin), raja of Yala, both died. Tuan Timung, son of Tuan Kundur, was appointed to become the raja in Rahman, with the title Phraya Rattanaphakdi. It was this raja who moved and made his village at present-day Kota Baharu Rahman. In Yala, Tungku Sulaiman (Tuan Kechik), son of Tungku Mahmud Salih, was appointed to become raja replacing his father and bearing the title Phraya Narongritphakdi. Thus too in the province at Nongchik, after the death of its raja named Nia Keliam, a Siamese chief named Nia Wing became Raja there with the title Phraya Pichera Pibul Narubit.

After this, Tungku Jeladaladin (Nik Lebai), raja of Sia, and Tuan Timung, raja of Rahman, also died. Tungku Abdul Kadir (Nik Kelapik), son of Tungku Jelaludin, became raja of the province of Sia, and was given the title Phraya Suriyasunthon Bowonphakdi, and Tungku Abdul Muta'ib (Nik Pik) was appointed to become his aide and given the title Phraya Rattanamontri. It was this Tungku Abdul Kadir who established the royal palace in Selindong Bayu or Teluban which still exists today.

In the province of Rahman, Tungku Abdul Kendis (Tuan Jangong), younger brother of Tuan Timong, was appointed to become raja, with the title Phraya Rattanaphakdi. Tuan Bali Jawa, son of Tuan Timong, and Tuan Lebih, son of Tungku Abdul Kendis, were both appointed to become his aides.*

---

*Previous to this, the rajas of the seven provinces of Patani were only given the title of Phraya. For example, the raja of Patani was titled Phraya Tani, the raja of Yala was titled Phraya Yala, and so forth. From this time the rajas were distinguished with individual titles: the raja of Patani was titled Phraya Wichitphakdi; the raja of Nongchik was titled Phraya Phetcharaphiban; the raja of Yala was titled Phraya Narongrit Si Prathet Winetwangsa; the raja of Sia was titled Phraya Suriayasonthan

Tungku Putih continued to rule Patani securely and peacefully. At the beginning of A.D. 1881, his majesty died after occupying the throne of the kingdom of Patani for twenty-six years. During his lifetime, his majesty had had two wives, namely: in Kelantan he had married Tungku Raja Puteri, the daughter of the sultan of Kelantan; in Patani he had married Tungku Wawah Puteri, daughter of Tungku Tengah who became advisor to the raja (Phraya Pitek). His majesty died of an illness while in Kelantan, and is remembered as Almarhum Mangkat di Kelantan.[78]

At his death his majesty left one son and six daughters,[79] namely:

From his Kelantan wife,
(1) Tungku Besar (Tungku Timung), the third raja of Patani;
(2) Tungku Ambung, wife of the Raja Bendahara of Kelantan;
From his Patani wife,
(3) Tungku Ambik, wife of Tungku Mahmud of Kelantan;
(4) Tungku Tengah, wife of the raja of Yala;
(5) Tungku Pik, wife of Tungku Mahmud, son of the raja of Belat;
(6) Tungku Patani, wife of Tungku Besar Indera, raja of Kelantan;
(7) Tungku Mahmud, who became raja muda in the government of Tungku Sulaiman Sharif Aladin.

When Tungku Putih died his son Tungku Besar (Tungku Timung) was appointed to occupy the throne of the kingdom of Patani and became the third raja. Also at that time no one had yet been appointed to fill the office of advisor to the raja. After the death of the raja of Banggul, Tungku Tengah, son of the raja of Banggul was appointed to become advisor to the raja, and

---

Bowonphakdi; the raja of Rahman was titled Phraya Phuphaphakdi; the raja of Ligeh was titled Phraya Phuphaphakdi; and the raja of Jering was titled Phraya Phiphitphakdi. These titles were used officially until, in the year A.D. 1902, the sovereignty and authority of the Malay rajas were abolished by the Siamese kingdom.

Tungku Sulaiman became raja muda. Tungku Abdul Kadir, son of Tungku Tengah, was appointed as an assistant to the raja.

Meanwhile Nai Wiang, raja of Nongchik, died and was replaced by a Siamese named Nia Ming who was given the title Phraya Phetcharaphiban. Not long afterward Nik Timun, raja of Jering, also died. His younger brother Nik Mah was appointed to become the raja ruling there and was given the title Phraya Phiphitsenamattayathibodi. Afterward, Nai Ming, raja of Nongchik, and Nik Bongsu, raja of Ligeh, also died. Nai Tud was appointed to become raja in Nongchik. Tuan Indu, son of Nik Bongsu, was appointed to become raja of Ligeh with the title Phraya Phuphaphakdi.

Tungku Besar (Tuan Timung) had occupied the throne of the kingdom of Patani for nine years and was the third raja of Patani to rule under the control of the raja of Siam-Thai. Because Patani at that time had fallen under the subjugation of the Siam-Thai raja, the question of the safety of the country from attacks by its enemies was no longer an issue. Thus, during the period of Tungku Besar's reign, in Patani there occurred no conflict either with enemies outside the country of with its enemies within the country itself, that is with the Siam-Thai.

In A.D. 1890 Tungku Besar died and was buried in a cemetery (Tok Ayah) which still exists today. At this death, his majesty left two sons and three daughters together with his three wives, Che Wah, Mek Putih, and Che Mek Inche Tih. Children by his wife Che Wah were (1) Tungku Besar, wife of the raja muda of Kelantan; (2) Tungku Wawah, wife of Tungku Hussein (Tungku Besar Nayara). His child by Mek Putih was (3) Tungku Mek Haji (Tungku Ismail).[80] Children by his wife Che Mek Inche Tih were (4) Tungku Tengah, wife of Tungku Nga, son of the raja of Sia; (5) Tungku Mahmud (Tungku Che Kumat).

After Tungku Besar died, Tungku Sulaiman Syarifalludin, the raja muda, was appointed to ascend the throne of the kingdom of Patani with the title Sultan Sulaiman Syarifalludin. He became the fourth raja during the period of Siam-Thai subjugation, and was titled by the Siam-Thai as Phraya Wichitphakdi.

Then Tungku Mahmud, son of Tungku Besar, was appointed to become raja muda. At that time Tungku Tengah, who held the position of advisor to the raja (Phraya Phakdi), also died and was replaced by his son, Tungku Abdul Kadir. Tungku Abdul Kadir, son of Sulaiman, was appointed to become assistant to the raja (Phraya Phiphitphakdi).

During his reign Sultan Sulaiman Syarifalludin was very concerned about the safety of the lives of the Patani people. Among his acts was the straightening of the Sungai Patani, which required excavation from Kampung Perigi as far as Kampung Anak Buloh. It length was approximately seven kilometers, and is known now by the name of Sungai Baru.

Besides this, his majesty took very seriously Islamic religious affairs. At his wish a large mosque was built of stone which is known by the name "Great Mosque of Chabang Tiga," and exists to this day. His Majesty Sultan Sulaiman Syarifalludin did not pray in the palace which was built previously by Almarhum Raja of Kelantan. Instead, his majesty built a new palace on the side of the city where the sun rose. In it his majesty prayed until [the day] he died, and this new palace became the place of prayer of Tungku Mahmud, the raja muda.

Not many years later Wan Induk, the raja of Ligeh, died and Tuan Tengah, his relative, that is the son of Tuan Sulong, was appointed to become raja of Ligeh in his place. Thus also when Nik Mah, raja of Jering, died, his son Nik Wawa was appointed to become raja to rule there.

Sultan Sulaiman Syarifalludin ruled with impartial justice and his majesty was very devoted to the people and the kingdom of Patani. Although his majesty's rule was carried out under the control and supervision of the Siam-Thai raja, nevertheless he upheld the position of his people, country, and kingdom.

After Sultan Sulaiman Syarifalludin had occupied the throne of the kingdom of Patani for ten years, to the beginning of A.D. 1899, on the fourth of the month of Rabi'ul-awwal 1316, his majesty also died and was buried in the cemetery of Tok Ayah.

On his death his majesty left two sons and two daughters which were borne by two wives, namely:

His child by his Kelantan wife,
(1) Tungku Sulung, wife of Tungku Betara.
His children by Tungku Nik Putih, daughter of the Raja of Sia,

(2) Tungku Besar Tuan Kambing, wife of Tungku Mahmud, the raja muda;
(3) Tungku Abdulkadir Kamaralladin, who later became the fifth raja of Patani,
(4) Tungku Mahmud Saleh.

After the death of his majesty, his son Tungku Abdulkadir Kamaralladin was chosen to ascend the throne of the kingdom of Patani in place of his father, and became the fifth raja of Patani descended from the rajas of Kelantan. He was also the last Malay raja to rule the country of Patani.

In the year A.D. 1902, the Siam-Thai raja in Bangkok decided to change the system of government in his subject territory of Patani. He wanted the seven provinces in Patani to be combined into a single province, called a region [*boriwen*]. He abolished the sovereignty and authority of the seven Malay rajas and placed the government of the country of Patani under the supervision and control of the raja of Singgora.

The Siam-Thai raja well knew that this wish would certainly be resisted strongly by the Malay rajas because this meant withdrawing their sovereignty and their right of overlordship in the country of Patani. Therefore he sent a minister as envoy to Patani in order to discuss this matter with the Malay rajas. In this meeting he requested the signatures of the Malay rajas as a token of permission and agreement with the wish of the raja of Siam. At the same time he promised to give pensions to the rajas and their households until their deaths. However, the rights and revenues in the country of Patani all had to be surrendered to the raja of Siam in Bangkok. The Malay rajas would no longer be forced to send tribute of the *bunga mas* to Bangkok.

By using all sorts of trickery and deceit many of the Malay rajas were deceived so that they were willing to give their signatures admitting agreement with the wishes of the raja of Siam-Thai. Only Tungku Abdulkadir Kamaralludin, raja of Patani, staunchly resisted the wishes of the raja of Siam and did not want to give his signature to the envoy from Siam who came to Patani. This was because his majesty knew that the desire of the raja of Siam meant the seizing of all rights of the Malay people, including the right of suzerainty over the country of Patani, and that the fate of the Malays would be to fall under the yoke of subjugation to the Siam-Thai, having lost their rights to freedom and independence.

With this realization, Tungku Abdulkadir was fully determined not to agree to the wish of the raja of Siam-Thai. At this the ministerial envoy tried forcibly to arrest his majesty. One day he pretended to invite his majesty to the house where he was staying. He said he wanted to discuss many things. As soon as his majesty came to his house he was quickly confined by the Siam-Thai men in a room and not permitted to leave. This affair was so quickly carried out that his majesty himself did not realize what was happening.

When the fact of his capture was known to the Malay chiefs they came in a crowd intending to free their raja from the captivity of the Siamese. But his majesty thought it useless to allow his people to spill their blood because he knew the strength of the people of Patani at that time was too small. So they left his majesty in captivity. The other Malay rajas agreed with the Siam-Thai raja by giving their signatures, except for the raja of Ligeh and the raja of Rahman, who were of the same opinion as his majesty. However, because they were threatened by the Siam-Thai, these rajas too later were forced to accede to the wishes of the raja of Siam.

Afterward the ministerial envoy of Siam returned to Bangkok, taking with him Tungku Abdulkadir Kamaralludin with the hope of urging or threatening his majesty to give his signature and agree with the wishes of the raja of Siam. But his majesty was a Malay raja of stout heart and greatly valued the sovereignty of the kingdom of Patani. He steadfastly resisted the wish of the raja of Siam-Thai. Then his majesty was sent to a place of confinement in the country of Phitsanulok, north of the city of Bangkok. Then many among the Malays of Patani who were loyal to his majesty resolved to go together to Phitsanulok. Some of them died on the way and some of them died there.

After two years and nine months during which his majesty was confined there, in A.D. 1905, his majesty received permission from the raja of Siam to return to Patani. At that time the system of government in the country of Patani had changed and altered according to the wishes of the Siam-Thai raja. The country of Patani had been combined into one province and was placed under the control and command of the raja of Singgora, and was ruled by a Siamese commissioner named Phraya Mahibanborirak, who lived in the country of Patani. All six rajas had lost their sovereignty and authority. Each lived only on his pension until the end of their lives.

After the return of Tungku Abdulkadir Kamaralludin to Patani, his majesty no longer wanted to stay in Patani and immediately set off to live in Kelantan for a few years, until in A.D. 1933 his majesty died of bronchitis in Kelantan.

At his death his majesty left three sons and three daughters:[81]

(1) Tungku Ahmad Nuraladdin (Tungku Sri Akar Raja Kelantan);

By Tuan Namsa,

(2) Tungku Zubaidah (Tungku Besar);
(3) Tungku Yusuf Shamsaladdin;
(4) Tungku Todzah, married to Raja Haji Ahmad of Perak,
(5) Tungku Kamarih:

By Che Manuk Patani,

(6) Tungku Yah, married to Tungku Abdulkadir (Tungku Putera), child of the Raja of Sia;
(7) Tungku Mahmud Mahialaddin.

Thus, A.D. 1902 was the year of the ultimate fall of the country of Patani, the loss of the sovereignty of its rajas, the destruction of the right of suzerainty of the Malays in the country of Patani, and the pawning of all rights to liberty and independence to the raja of Siam-Thai. This was the last and most unfortunate year in the history of the fall of the Malay kingdom of Patani.

With the death of Tungku Abdulkadir Kamaralludin, the Malay rajas from the line of Kelantan rajas who occupied the throne of the kingdom of Patani were no more. From that time no one was elevated to become raja of Patani. The country of Patani had begun to be just one of the provinces subject to the Siam-Thai kingdom.

In A.D. 1906, also upon the wish of the raja of Siam, the government was dissolved and replaced by a newer method of government. All seven provinces in Patani were reunited in one provincial territory of Patani, in the Siamese language termed "*monton* Patani." Then the province of Patani was again divided into four territories which were called *changwat*, that is the changwat of Patani, Yala, Saiburi, and Narathiwat (Banganara). Then a Siam-Thai commissioner was appointed to rule in each changwat.

A high commissioner (governor-general) was appointed and stationed in Patani, to govern the four provinces, and all the commissioners in each province governed under his supervision. The high commissioner was called, in the Siamese language, Samuha Thetsaphiban. The Siamese who first held this post of high commissioner in the province of Patani was named Phraya Sakseninarong, and his new titled was Phraya Dechanuchi.

Chapter 4

THE COUNTRY OF PATANI IN THE
PERIOD OF REAWAKENING

After the sovereignty of the Malay rajas of Patani was abolished through trickery by the Siamese kingdom in 1902, the country of Patani was gradually absorbed as a part of the territory of the country of Siam-Thai and its Patani Malay subjects were changed to citizens of the state of Siam-Thai. Siamese officials who came from the Bangkok region began to take up posts in Patani. Their method of administration in the country of Siam-Thai at that time was conducted through rule by the authority of the raja (autocracy). Thus the pattern of government in Patani stressed the advantages and benefits for these Siamese officials and their kingdom.

The Malays were made subject to and forced to pay maximum taxes as revenue to the kingdom. As far as possible all the wealth of Patani was to be collected and all the revenue thus collected was to be sent to Bangkok. A small part was put aside to pay the salaries of the Siamese officials. It may be said that no one part of the revenue was used for the welfare of the Malays who had strained to pay the tax.

The majority of the Siamese officials never seriously considered the welfare of the Malays. They first came to Patani with only their official rank. But when they retired they had obtained many broad estates and large compounds in Patani. Some of them, when they retired, returned to Bangkok taking possessions to make their lives luxurious. The officials of Siam-Thai never tried to understand the Malay people and the Islamic religion, because in the period of autocratic rule there was no such concern. They ruled with great ease, but were unconcerned with

79

progress in these territories except for affairs concerning their own advantage.

Services of health, education, and welfare did not exist; Siamese schools were established only in the city, for the benefit of children of Siamese officials. There were no Malay schools. When the government wanted roads to facilitate communications between one territory and another, they depended on local people to build them. They were mobilized to work as laborers. Sometimes laborers were forced to come from their home miles away and were forced to bring their own supplies.

The administration of judicial matters depended on the high commissioner, on the police, and finally on the judges. Sometimes people brought to court were forced to wait for months before their case came to trial. This state of affairs was caused by officials who wanted to find out how much money would be given to them by an accused person when their case came to trial. Such a system of administration made the Malays feel restless and dissatisfied.

In 1923 the Malays started a movement by refusing to pay tax because of their hatred of the Siam-Thai officials who received their money and also because their system of administration did nothing to improve the country. In this year the Malays launched a movement to demand freedom. This movement was suppressed by the kingdom of Siam after a fight occurred between members of the movement and a troop of Siamese police in the district of Mayul (Rakak). Several Malay leaders accused of involvement in this movement were arrested and sent to Bangkok charged with treason. Some of them died and were buried there.

Among the Malay leaders who directed the movement was Tungku Abdulkadir Kamaralludin, the last raja of Patani, who had refused the offer of the Siamese kingdom to become a puppet raja. After the movement began to break up his majesty withdrew to Kelantan and stayed there permanently until he died.[82]

Because this event occurred, and because he was too old, Phraya Dechanuchit, high commissioner for the province (monton) of Patani, was withdrawn from office and replaced by another person. The occupant of this post changed several times until 1932. In this year the country of Siam was ruled by Raja

Prajadhipok, the seventh of his line, and the economic situation of the country of Siam declined so far as to endanger the kingdom.

With the aim of reversing the collapse of the economy of the kingdom of Siam, methods of internal administration were greatly altered, including a decreased number of officials and a cutback on plans for unimportant expenditures. Several provinces throughout the country of Siam were eliminated, one of which was the province of Patani, which was abolished and combined with the province of Nakhom Sri Thammarat. And in Patani one district was abolished, the Saiburi (Teluban) district. Half of it was combined with Patani district and half was combined with Narathiwat district. Then there remained only three districts, Patani, Yala, and Narathiwat. And all three were under the rule of the high commissioner of the province of Nakhon Sri Thammarat, centered in Singgora.

Steps to reverse the economic collapse were implemented without much success. The politicians felt their country would slip into poverty and the number of unemployed people would increase. Therefore on the morning of 24 June 1932 a revolt occurred which seized power and Bangkok was controlled by politicians called "The Peoples' Association" consisting of officers of the army, navy, and air force, together with civilians. Their aim was to change the autocratic style of government to a democratic style of government (sovereignty of the people). This association was led by Phraya Pahun, Nai Pridi Panum Yong, Luang Phibunsongkhram and others, including leaders of the Islamic community in Bangkok such as Haji Abdulwahab and Haji Shamsalladin Mustapi.

Afterwards a new constitution was promulgated and implemented according to democratic methods, giving an opportunity to the people of every district to exercise their right to choose a representative to attend a council of the kingdom in Bangkok, as people's representatives who were responsible and had the right to become involved in affairs of the government of the kingdom. The formerly unlimited sovereignty of the raja of Siam was restricted by the constitution, and the democratic kingdom of Siam was permanently established. Then five principles of the government of the country were promulgated as basic acts of democracy which were:[83]

(1) To ensure political, judicial, and economic independence;
(2) To ensure safety and calm in the country;
(3) To advance the prosperity of the common people;
(4) To give equal rights to the common people;
(5) To provide sufficient education for the common people.

In 1933 the Siam-Thai kingdom abolished all provides (monton) in the country of Siam and retained only districts (changwat), and all districts including the Districts of Patani, Yala, and Bangenara were made directly subject to rule by the Ministry of the Interior in Bangkok. With this last change the country of Patani essentially had become an integral part of the country of Siam-Thai, and its condition became increasingly separated from the other Malay countries in the peninsula.

In the new constitutional arrangement, it was stated in the first sentence that "the country of Siam-Thai is one in all aspects and may not be divided." With the democratic form of government in existence, the Malays in the districts mentioned felt a sense of hope upon hearing the proclamations of democracy which sounded so sweet, and each awaited the opportunity to express the spirit of democracy which gave equal rights and freedom. But from year to year there was no change at all, particularly in matters of health, education, roads, and others. All these were neglected as in the previous period of autocracy. Again the Malays felt restless and dissatisfied.

However, the democratic form of government caused the Siamese to become increasingly nationalistic, more than before. The Siamese interpreted the first sentence of the constitution to mean that every person who is a Siam-Thai subject must be counted as a Siamese in everything, that all must use one language, set of customs, similar clothes, and one religion. They had forgotten that in the constitution there also was one sentence which guaranteed freedom of religion, custom, and way of life to all people who live in the country of Siam.

In 1939 Thai nationalism had begun to spread in the country of Siam, spurred by Luang Phibunsongkhram, who at that time had become prime minister. Among the chief men of Siam, Luang Phibunsongkhram was famous as a strong politician who made much use of nationalism. He had many plans to develop nationalism throughout all the provinces of Indochina. He also intended to suppress minority groups in his country.

In 1940 a Siamese Cultural Institute was established in Bangkok and was known by the name "Sapha Wattanatham," the goal of which was the advancement of nationalism and the expansion of Siamese culture throughout the country. This Cultural Institute gradually issued directives in the form of compulsory rules for the public. One of the first directives which was issued compelled all people of Siam to wear Western-style clothing, including hats for both men and women. At meals it was necessary to use spoons and forks and to sit on chairs at a table. Malays in the districts of Patani, Yala, Narathiwat, and Setul felt this directive was aimed directly at them because they were forbidden to wear Malay clothing, use Malay names, speak the Malay language, and embrace the Islamic religion.

Among a few requirements of the rules advancing Siamese culture, it was forbidden to speak Malay in any government office. Government officers who knew Malay were strictly forbidden to speak Malay with local inhabitants. Malays who came to settle a matter in an office of the kingdom were forced to use the Siamese language. If they did not speak Siamese they were forced to hire someone who knew Siamese to be their interpreter, whether the affair was important or not.

Among the requirements advancing Thai culture, it also was stated that Buddhism was the official religion, that Islam must be opposed, and that every effort which would advance Islam must be inhibited. Even worse, some Malay people in the district of Saiburi (Teluban) were forced to pray to an idol of Buddha. Thus Buddhist idols were installed in Siamese schools and the pupils, a majority of whom were Malay children, were forced to pray to them.[84] A small number of Malays who held offices in the kingdom were forced to change their names to Siamese and it was forbidden for Malays to hold high offices. People who were Muslims were forbidden to attend military schools and hold higher offices.

In 1942 the cultural regulations were gradually implemented in the Malay districts, forcing Malays to wear Western clothes: coat, trousers, and hats for men, and tight blouses and short skirts for women. Anyone refusing to follow regulations was arrested and fined, and sometimes kicked and beaten by the Siamese police. In this year the Malays in those districts became restless, especially the religious teachers. They too were forced to wear Western clothing and often the robes and turbans of the Hajis were snatched off by the Siamese police and trampled under their feet. Similarly women, while buying and selling in Malay markets, were kicked and jabbed with gun butts by the Siamese police because they wore long loose dresses and shawls.

Thus, because of the proposals of Luang Phibunsongkhram, the Siamese officials in Malay districts were able to terrorize unchecked everywhere, supported by the cultural regulations. They became more and more zealous in desecrating the honor of the Islamic religion and Malay custom, and their nationalism caused them to feel scorn and contempt for the Malays.

On 8 December 1942 war broke out in East Asia when Japanese troops launched their attack in areas of Southeast Asia. Among their attacks were landings on all the east coast of Siam, including Patani. The Japanese troops attacked all along the eastern border of Siam and fighting with Siamese troops went on for several hours. Luang Phibunsongkhram violated his neutral status by permitting Japanese troops to pass through the country of Siam to extend their attacks against Burma and Malaya. With this step Luang Phibunsongkhram caused Malaya and Singapore to fall into the hands of Japan with ease. Not many days later he declared war on the other side and faithfully worked together with Japan. During the war the movement to advance Siamese culture and nationalism broadened and an agreement was reached between the Siamese Cultural Institute and the Japanese Cultural Institute in order to assist in advancing each culture.

Using military strength and an iron fist, Luang Phibunsongkhram succeeded in maintaining high power in government and, sheltered under the samurai sword, he began to implement dictatorial rule and imitate the actions of the Fascists. During the rule of the dictator Phibunsongkhram, the acts of the Siamese officials toward the Malays became increasingly highhanded and cruel and the movement to "Siamize" the Malays became increasingly clear. The second step began to be implemented, that is the building up of the grandeur of Siam based on the concept of Greater Siam. On this basis, the dictator Phibunsongkhram sent a troop of his soldiers to subjugate the Shan districts in Burma and in 1943 entered to govern within Kelantan, Trengganu, Perlis, and Kedah.

In the year 1944, Phibunsongkhram abolished the office of religious magistrate in the districts of Patani, Yala, Narathiwat, and Setul, and revoked Islamic laws concerning marriage, divorce, and inheritance which had been recognized by the kingdom of Siam for decades. Subsequently all cases pertaining to Islamic affairs were forced to follow the civil laws of the kingdom and were settled by Siamese courts.

In this year the situation of the Malays and the honor of the Islamic religion became increasingly endangered. In the same year, theologians led by Haji Sulung bin Abdul Kadir established an Islamic organization in Patani called *He'et alNapadh alLahkan alShariat* with the object of encouraging cooperation among Islamic leaders responsible for resisting the movement of the kingdom of Siam to Siamize the Malays and to violate the Islamic religion.

On the 14th day of January 1944, which coincides with the Siamese year 2487, a request was sent to the Prime Minister Phibunsongkhram by Tungku Abdul Jalal bin Tungku Abdul Talib, a leader of the Malays in southern Siam who was motivated by genuine loyalty to his people and was the Malay representative in the Siamese parliament at that time. This request concerned enforcement of the Siamese cultural regulations with regard to the culture of the Malay people in southern Siam and the desecration of the religion of Islam, which was being carried out by the governor of Patani (a Siam-Thai). An official reply was finally received on the 29th of April 1944, coinciding with the Siamese year 2487. This reply came from the Office of the Secretary of the Prime Minister Phibunsongkhram and expressed approval of the behavior of the governor of Patani and the manner in which he carried out the tyrannical Siamese cultural regulations, which were so crude and forceful. The letter read: "I wish to make known to you that your letter dated 14/2/1944 concerning the actions of the governor of Patani has been examined, and the Office of the Ministry of the Interior has given notice that the actions of the Governor of Patani are considered to be proper and

85

should give no cause for anger from the majority of the people. Be so informed."[85]

This was the only answer of the government of Phibunsongkhram to the protest of the Malays and the Islamic congregation in southern Siam voiced by their leader. This protest did not receive fair consideration. On the contrary, the government of Siam approved the behavior of its cruel and tyrannical officials. On the 14th of August, Japan surrendered to the Allies and the war of Greater East Asia ended. The dictator Phibunsongkhram was arrested as a war criminal in Siam due to his cooperation with the Japanese and was put into a Siamese jail for six months.

With the victory of the Allies, the goal of establishing Greater Siam was no longer attainable and efforts to spread Siamese culture were halted. In the month of August 1945, Nai Khuana Aphaiwong was selected to become prime minister of Siam and a new cabinet of ministers was formed. The government of Nai Kuang abolished all of the culture laws made by Phibunsongkhram and the movement to Siamize the Malays stopped.

Even so, the cruelty and violations of Siamese officials against the Malays did not cease. The sensibilities of the Siamese officials were ruined so that laws of justice and humanity were discarded. At this time there was a sort of contagious disease among the Siamese officials which led to disregard of directives and the taking of bribes. This occurred from the highest officials to the lowest peons. A matter that was very important could not succeed if bribes to the officials were not first prepared.

With the police, a criminal who was caught could with ease be safe and free if he gave them a bribe. Repeatedly, when a Malay was accused of friendship with bad elements, he was immediately arrested by the Siamese police, taken to a lonely place, and beaten before he was taken to the place of detention. This also happened to Malays accused of taking part in political movements critical of the government. They were always threatened and slandered in various ways by the Siamese police, arrested, or simply beaten without bothering to take the matter to court.

In the month of December 1947, a tragic and horrible event occurred in Patani when a Siamese police bailiff was shot to death by bandits near a village named Kampung Belukar Masahak. A force of Siamese police went to this village to arrest Malay youths and proceeded to torture them in various ways in order to find out who among them was the murderer. They charged that the Malay youths in that village were supplying provisions to bandits, giving them full assistance. Many Siamese police came and burned the village because it was charged that the residents of the village were befriending the bandits. With this fire twenty-five Malay families were made homeless.

On the 26th of September 1947 Miss Barbara Wittingham-Jones, an English reporter, visited Patani for the first time since the end of the war. She traveled through 250 miles of the country in order to study and observe the condition of the 700,000 Malays under the oppression of the kingdom of Siam.

In the newspaper *Straits Times*, from Singapore, in the issue of December 1, Miss [Wittingham-] Jones told of her investigation. In her words: "Wherever I went, I found principles of oppression applied in an organized manner and an intentional movement launched to Siamize the subjects of the country.[86] The opinion of the public has been disregarded by enforced prohibition by the kingdom of Siam regarding education for the Malays there," said Miss [Wittingham-] Jones, while explaining that schools in Patani had been closed by the Thai kingdom of Siam.

> All along the way I saw school buildings closed and empty. Even religious schools were prohibited by the kingdom of Siam, although one or two Malay schools were still open, mainly in Yala and Narathiwat. But during one or two days of my visit there, a few more were forced to close. Because the Malays do not want to send their children to Siamese schools and are stubborn about not wanting to study the Siamese language, the decline of education among the Malay people in Patani is holding back their social and economic progress.

Stating that this Siamese principle has killed the life and spirit of the Malay people, Miss [Wittingham-] Jones explained that the result is a gulf separating "the Siamese subjects and the Malays, which grows wider every day." The Siamese colonist, she says further, looks with obvious distaste and contempt on the Malay subjects, characterizing the Malay subjects as a race of illiterate and stupid farmers.

"As a pariah among social groups, it is not surprising if some of the more stubborn Malays become enemies of society, by becoming pirates on land and sea," Miss [Wittingham-] Jones says. "Every level of Siamese officials take bribes and because this evil is further compounded by the feelings of the Siamese officials who look with distaste and contempt on the Malays, the fate of the Patani Malays is to suffer constant tyranny and oppression, the basis for their desire for revenge on the Siamese officials." Then Miss [Wittingham-] Jones relates how the Siamese police burned Malay villages to the ground because those villages were accused of protecting criminals. "The Siamese police did not wish to investigate the truth or falsehood of those accusations or to try the people in court. Siamese officials have entered Malay homes to rape Malay women and force Malay shops to pay protection money. That protection money totals thousands of *tikal* and Siamese police often enter Malay shops to steal whatever they want," Miss [Wittingham-] Jones said further.[87]

To demonstrate that the lives of Patani Malays were cheap the reporter says "Malays are often summarily shot without further investigation or mysteriously disappear without leaving a trace or further reports. Because Patani is isolated from the outside world, the Malays cannot and do not constitute an opposition to this harsh and cruel government. Simple dissention against the Siamese rule is considered by the kingdom of Siam to endanger the safety of the country. Such dissention is crushed by death sentences or torture. Malays in Patani are not free to speak, have no newspapers, have few radios, and no political organization. The place used by the Patani Malays to raise their voices are the mosques. Occasionally a Malay newspaper is smuggled to Patani, the *Utusan Melayu* newspaper [of Malaya].

Furthermore Miss [Wittingham-] Jones explains: "Although Thai Siam has oppressed the Patani Malays so terribly for fifty years, nevertheless the principle of Siamizing Malays in Patani has not yet succeeded. I was surprised to see the spiritual strength of the Patani Malays in withstanding oppression so that they are able to preserve their culture."

Thus the summary of the facts by which the reporter Miss [Wittingham-] Jones portrays the situation actually prevailing in the Malay districts of southern Siam. From this can be understood the reasons why the Patani Malays have simultaneously arisen and asked for independence and justice.

The news of cruelty and the efforts to Siamize the Malays of Patani caused a commotion throughout the world, especially in Malaya. In the month of August 1947 the kingdom of Siam sent a commission consisting of seven people to Patani in order to investigate these matters and to listen to the local inhabitants in order to bring about a change that would be suitable to the Malays.

On the 24th of August the investigatory commission held a general meeting with the Malays of Patani which provided an opportunity for questions and answers. In this meeting Haji Sulung bin Abdul Kadir, the head of the Islamic Council, and Wan Othman Ahmad, head of the *Persekutuan Semangat Patani* [Alliance of the Spirit of Patani], represented the populace of Patani, and submitted to the commission seven demands to be presented to the government.[88] The contents of the demands were:

(1) The government of Siam should have a person of high rank possessing full power to govern the four provinces of Patani, Yala, Narathiwat, and Setul, and this person should be a Muslim born within one of the provinces and elected by the populace. The person in this position should be retained without being replaced;

(2) All of the taxes obtained within the four provinces should be spent only within the provinces;

(3) The government should support education in the Malay medium up to the fourth grade in parish schools within the four provinces;

89

(4) Eighty percent of the government officials within the four provinces should be Muslims born within the provinces;

(5) The government should use the Malay language within government offices alongside the Siamese language;

(6) The government should allow the Islamic Council to establish laws pertaining to the customs and ceremonies of Islam with the agreement of the [above noted] high official;

(7) The government should separate the religious court from the civil court in the four provinces and permit [the former] full authority to conduct cases.

The letter containing these demands made clear the deeds of the local Siamese officials who often indecently abrogated the rights of the Malay populace, and attempted to persuade the Siam-Thai government that their demands were not contrary to the constitution of the kingdom of Siam, rather that they [the demands] were directed toward improving the fate of their people and their homeland in a time when the world is busy preparing important rights and freedoms for the peoples who have been colonized.

In analyzing the problems faced by the Malay populace in conjunction with these demands it was stated:

We the Malay people realize that the true reality of our condition under the government of Siam is indecent and miserable whenever we are called Thai Islam. With such an appellation it is made clear that the question of our nationality as Malay people is not recognized by the kingdom of Siam. Because of this, we, in the name of all of the Malay common people in Patani, unanimously demand that the kingdom of Siam consider us as Malay people of the Islamic religion so that no longer will the world view us as Thai Islam.

The Siamese government investigating team heard all of the demands of the Patani Malays and it was agreed that the demands would be forwarded to the government in Bangkok.

At the same time it was reported that the Malays in the province of Narathiwat also had proposed similar demands to the same investigating team. Their demands were made by fifty-five local Malay leaders. Among their demands was that the Siamese Office of Broadcasting in Bangkok should have a portion of their broadcast in the Malay language every day. Offices of the government should close on Fridays as the day of rest and also on Islamic religious holidays. The system of education should be changed to accord with the standards of the modern world. Under the direction of Muslim officials, taxes obtained from the four provinces should be applied to the welfare of the four provinces. There were other demands contained in the thirteen points. Not many days later Malays from the province of Setul, represented by Incik Abdullah bin Mahmud Sa'ad, sent similar demands.

All of the demands of the Malay people were delivered to the Siamese government in Bangkok, but did not result in any changes from the Siamese government. Rather, Siamese officials were of the opinion that these demands were quite contrary to the national Constitution and need not be considered.

On the 30th of January 1948 a special correspondent of the *Utusan Melayu* in Bangkok asked the deputy prime minister of Siam what was the attitude of the government regarding these demands. He answered, "The demands will be considered punctually and as many of the demands as possible will be implemented." This reply meant that the Malay demands which did not hinder the operations of the Siamese government would be implemented, but that whichever conflicted with their proprieties would be rejected. Some members of the Siamese government interpreted the demands as a political movement against the constitutional laws, and thought that it was necessary to take strong action against the Malays.

By order of the Siamese commissioner of Patani, on the morning of the 16th of January 1948, a troop of armed Siamese police arrested Haji Sulung at his house and two days later arrested Wan Othman Ahmad, Haji Wan Hussein, and Wan Mahmud Ami. The Malay leaders who had voted the demands of the Malay people were arrested and accused of treason against the kingdom. One month later Haji Sulung and his colleagues were taken to Nakhon Sri Thammarat, and the Siamese court there concluded their deliberations by imposing jail sentences of three years. Two months later they were taken to Bangkok and detained in the large prison "Bang Kwang."

After these arrests, many Malays of Patani who also were accused of involvement in the movement fled to seek refuge in Malaya. The Islamic Council of Patani was outlawed by the government. During this year all activities of the Patani Malays were constantly watched by the Siamese government, and many special undercover agents were sent from Bangkok to Patani, Yala, and Narathiwat to investigate the activities of those Malays who were considered to be political and opposed to the government, or who demanded freedom.

The Malay question became a regular subject in the discussions of the members of the Siamese government. Moreover, their problems caused a commotion in Malaya when Malay newspapers stood up in support of the Malay movements in southern Siam. *Utusan Melayu*, the most important Malay newspaper, stood up for and supported their aspirations. The voice of *Utusan Melayu* constantly criticized the members of the Siamese government and its voice resounded in the Siamese parliament when the condition of the Malays, who suffered behind the Siamese iron curtain [*tabir besi*], was made known.

During this time a group of conservative Siamese newspapers who supported the government constantly slandered the endeavors of the Malay people while calling their movement wicked. There also were honest Siamese newspapers who honored the principles of the press and were sympathetic to the Malays.

On the 30th of January 1948 a troop of special Siamese police were sent from Bangkok to the Malay provinces to reinforce the hold of the government over the Malay people, as it was believed that their movement would expand. On the 28th of April 1948, there occurred a fierce battle between one thousand Malays and a force of Siam-Thai police at Kampung Dusun Nyior in the province of Narathiwat. The Siamese police began the attack against the Malays, accusing the Malays of actions against the Siamese government. The battle lasted for thirty-six hours before the Malays retreated to the jungle to carry out a guerrilla struggle. Close to 400 Malays, including old people, women, and children, were killed in the battle, and more than thirty Siamese police were killed.

On the 27th of April, three Siamese bombers flew over the area of the battle to bomb the Malays.[89] Siamese warships harbored at Kuala Bengenara were ordered to land their troops to assist the Siamese police in killing the Malay people. One month later, *Kamnan* Mahmud, the headman of Kampung Tanjong Mas, and Mustaphi, and old Malay man of Telabuan, were arrested by the Siamese police and accused of involvement in the unrest. The two of them were killed without being given a hearing in court.[90]

The Siamese government tried to keep secret the events which led up to the battle and lied to the world by saying that it was simply a battle between a group of bandits and the guardians of peace. But the truth could not be hidden in the face of clear evidence that showed that the Malays had lost their patience and were increasingly dissatisfied with the Siam-Thai government. The sacrifice of hundreds of Malay lives was a major event in the history of the rising of the Malay people of Patani, who demand justice and freedom.

The government of Siam endeavored to blur the eyes of the world with their propaganda by belittling the Malay movement and stressing that the Malays acted because they were paid by a small group of Patani Malay agitators who had fled to Malaya.

To confront the propaganda of the Siamese government, on the 6th of February 1948, under the leadership of the head of a committee of Malay representatives in southern Siam, a protest was sent to the prime minister of Siam who had said that the Malay movement represented only a small faction of the Malays. The head of the committee also sent his protest to Lake Success, New York, asking that the United Nations take measures to carry out an investigation in Siam for the purpose of holding a plebiscite to determine the true condition and attitude of the Malays in southern Siam.[91]

Copies of the protest also were sent to the British and American embassies in Bangkok, noting the true condition of the

93

Malay movement. This protest demanded that the prime minister of Siam prove to the world the truth or falsity of the position of the kingdom of Siam by permitting a plebiscite headed by a representative of the United Nations, and without the presence of the Siamese troops and officials.

This protest was received by the government of Siam in Bangkok, but it was not considered, as on the 8th of December 1947 a *coup d'état* occurred in Bangkok.[92] Two months later Luang Phibunsongkhram, the former war criminal, became prime minister. On the 29th of January 1948, the government of Phibunsongkhram held an election to legitimize the government, and to obtain the recognition of foreign nations, especially world powers. The Malays of Patani began to boycott the election, not wanting to elect representatives to parliament because of the return of Lung Phibunsongkhram, which was not legitimate under the Constitution of the nation. They did not want to support the government of Phibunsongkhram, but the efforts of the Malays were unsuccessful because of the threats and intimidations of the Siamese police. Finally, Luang Phibunsongkhram returned to power in the government. With his return, the Malays were restless and dissatisfied because during the dictator's previous rule, Luang Phibunsongkhram had been a great enemy of the Malays.

With the return of Luang Phibunsongkhram the question arose among the Malays whether he would once again attempt to Siamize the Malays as he had before, or whether he would implement other measures. Several months later he re-established the Council of Culture and gradually began to implement the cultural laws of the past, which were compulsory. Beginning with the year 1950, the Chinese within Siam were bared from thirteen occupations, and there were reports that he would force the Malays to wear Western clothing once again. These matters troubled the Malays.

On the 10th of October 1949, at the invitation of the kingdom of Siam, a group of Malay news reporters representing Malay, English, Chinese, and Tamil newspapers were taken to visit the provinces of Patani, Yala, and Narathiwat, to observe and investigate the true condition of the Malays in southern Siam. Wherever they went they were constantly misled and spied upon

94

by the Siamese police. Their condition was the same as prisoners as they [the police] did not want to allow the reporters to meet and speak with the Malays and/or receive the true story.

Even though closed off and covered up by the government of Siam, the condition of the Malays in southern Siam has become clear to the world. Their life is one of constant sorrow and they receive no assistance from the Siam-Thai government. If studied in depth, since the fall of Patani in the eighteenth century until this day, it is clear that the government of Siam has misgoverned during this whole period of time. No progress has been made in Patani to provide well-being for the Malays. In matters of health, education, association, and economy, Patani has lagged far behind the progress of its neighbors in Malaya. The actions of the Siamese government which allow the Malays to live in backwardness, definitely gives a large profit to them, but this has grieved the hearts of the Malays. The Malays of Patani were forced to pawn their country to the government of Siam with the hope that they would be given good leadership toward general progress, or at the very least be allowed equality with the leadership given to the Siamese people. Patani is not poor, and has natural wealth in the land. Among the provinces of southern Siam, Patani should be counted as rich, with no need to depend on the wealth of the Siamese from other provinces to pay for the welfare of the Malays. If in the more than sixty years of Siamese rule in Patani only 50 percent of the taxes had been used for the welfare of the Malays, then surely this day Patani would appear in a better condition. At least the main roads of Patani would not be cart tracks and her towns would surely not be like the towns of the Sakai of Malaya.

The principles of democracy in Siam claim to provide equality and freedom, to assure adequate education to the people and certain other beautiful claims. But it has been seventeen years since democracy in Siam has been in effect, and no evidence is visible to the Malay people. Certainly there is progress in a period of democracy, as can be seen in the city of Bangkok, which is far more developed than ten years ago. The streets of the city have been made from concrete, hundreds of hospitals have been built, tens of institutions of higher education have been established, all aspects of the livelihood of the Siamese have been given assistance, and many kinds of useful guidance given to the

Siamese people. In Patani, democracy such as this appears not to have arrived and is unknown by the Malays in Patani. Siamese democracy apparently reaches only the area of Bangkok and the territory surrounding it. Siam-Thai democracy is for the Siam-Thai, for the religion of Buddha, for the oppression of the Malays, and for the violation of the religion of Islam. Truly peculiar is the Siamese democracy, and it is clear that democracy made in Siam is not fit for the Malay people.

Observing the condition of the world today, there arises one further question: is it the ultimate condition of the Patani Malays to be forever satisfied to live imprisoned under the conservative democracy of Siam? Today the world is moving to build a true understanding of democracy, under the grand principles of the United Nations at Lake Success, New York, to free the colonized peoples and implant feelings of democracy among all peoples, so that love of democracy enters their consciousness and it becomes their mutual responsibility to guard world security. When will the Patani Malays experience democracy and, once conscious of their fate, agree to struggle until the end for democracy? These questions are raised by the intellectuals of Patani's Malays today.

Among the one hundred million Malay people of the world, the Malays of Patani are the most ill-fated. Even though the Malay people of Patani long have lived in the democratic world, because Siam-Thai democracy is limited, the fate of the Malay people is like a climbing vine unable to grow up the trellis.

In truth the fate of the Patani Malay people should not be placed in the hands of the Siam-Thai government. Rather, measures to improve their fate and condition should be placed in their own hands.

TRANSLATORS' NOTES

Forward

1. See Teeuw and Wyatt's (1970) two volume translation of the *Hikayat Patani*. The history of Patani is summarized in Vol. I, pp. 1-24.

Author's Introduction

2. This is probably a copy of the *Hikayat Patani* translated by Teeuw and Wyatt (1970), as noted in the translators' introduction.

Chapter 1

3. *Tanah Melayu* literally means "Malay Land," and is used to refer to the Malay-inhabited southern half of the Malay Peninsula. The expression carries approximately the same sentimental connotation as "fatherland" in English, though the literal meaning is by no means equivalent. We have translated *Tanah Melayu* in much of the remainder of the text as "Malaya" where the term is used simply to denote a geographical location. Occasionally we have retained *Tanah Melayu* where it was used in an emotionally evocative manner.
4. The translation of Malay words for territorial units presents difficulties. These terms may have implications of size and political status which require an acquaintance with the complete structure of the ideal Malay polity and the

manifestations of this idea at different places and times. There are disputes among historians regarding the significance of some terms, which perhaps reflect ambiguity in the use of these terms by the Malays themselves. The following quote, which refers to Gullick's *Indigenous Political Systems of Western Malaya*, illustrates this point.

> Gullick seems to have used *daerah* and *jajahan* interchangeably. However, it would be more appropriate to view jajahan as an exclusive unit of a vassal or 'colony' in sultanic feudalistic sense. . . . The basic criterion for the distinction between daerah and jajahan is to be viewed from the fact that a jajahan could represent a unit bigger than a daerah or negeri. In the same context, a jajahan could also incorporate the whole of a territory of the sultan in question. (Chew Hock Tong 1974:131)

Numerous authorities have noted that the term "feudal" should not be applied to Malay society since the Malay polity was not primarily an expression of control over land; rather, successful Malay rulers sought to attract and keep loyal subjects as the basis of their prosperity. Size of population was more indicative of prosperity than size of area under a ruler's control. There is thus a basic conceptual inconsistency in using English terms, based on territorial polities, to translate Malay words for political divisions. At this point interested readers should consult Dobbin (1975:77-89) and Gullick (1965).

5. The term Siam-Thai can be translated as "ethnic Thai citizens in the territory of the kingdom of Siam." This term is used frequently in the text; Syukri probably intended to use this term to emphasize the fact that several distinct cultural groups made up the kingdom ruled by a Siamese monarch, of whom the Thai were only one. The term *Siam-Asli* (literally "aboriginal Siamese") is also used below, to

98

refer to non-Thai groups who he believes migrated south into present-day peninsular Malaysia to escape pressure from advancing Thai immigrants from southern China. The translators have left the terms for ethnic groups such as Siam-Thai and Siam-Asli untranslated since these are not ethnological terms in common use, but rather were created by Syukri for the purpose of conveying a specific meaning.

6. The word *bangsa* is another term with ethnic connotations which is difficult to translate into English. In the present work we have rendered it as "people" or "type of people." Most Malays consider linguistic and religious affiliation to be as important as genealogical origin in determinations of ethnicity. See D.E. Brown (1970) and Milner (1977).

7. See Note 5, above.

8. From a Malay perspective, "Sakai" as an ethnic term possesses derogatory connotations and is used to refer to a number of aboriginal groups of peninsular Malaysia. The Sakai groups are negritoid hunters and gatherers, and were sometimes captured and used as slaves by coastal Malays; thus, Sakai can mean slave.

9. *Zaman Jahiliah*, the period prior to the revelations of the will of Allah conveyed to his prophet Mohammad.

10. The term negeri derives from Sanskrit *nagari*, and in Southeast Asia has been used to designate entities ranging from villages in west Sumatra to states comprising the modern nation of Malaysia. In general, the term negeri implies the existence of an organized polity. Negeri could also be translated as "state" in the general sense of an area of territory with an independent ruler. See also note 4, above. We have translated negeri as "country," a mere general term we feel is consistent with the author's intent.

11. Tambralinga is mentioned in an inscription found near Ligor, as well as in Chinese records of the Sung Dynasty (960-1179), and in an inscription from Tapjou, South India, of the same period. It was probably in the Ligor area; see O'Connor (1975); Wheatley (1961:67); and Wolters (1958).

12. Gerahi is another small state of the early second millennium, located near Nakhon Sri Thammarat. It probably had been

absorbed by Tambralinga by A.D. 1280 (Coedes 1968:342, note 102).

13. Takkola is a port mentioned in the *Geography* attributed to the Greek geographer Ptolemy of the second century A.D., as well as Chinese and Indian sources of the seventh through fourteenth centuries. It probably was located somewhere on the northwest coast of the Malay peninsula (Wheatley 1961:252).

14. Langkasuka is called by Wheatley "one of the most intriguing of the early kingdoms of the Malay Peninsula." It is extensively described in Chinese and Arabic sources of the seventh and eighth centuries, which indicate a location in the region of Patani. The Javanese poem *Nagaraketagama* of A.D. 1365 also mentions Langkasuka, noting it was a tributary state of Majapahit. The *Hikayat Marong Mahawangsa* (Kedah Annals), however, places it on the west coast of the peninsula. Wheatley (1961:265) argues for Patani as its probable location, and notes that, "Emerging as an entity early in the period of Indianization, it persisted through the vicissitudes of peninsular history until early in the sixteenth century when it mysteriously disappeared, leaving only a legendary name to present mythology."

15. The *jawi* orthography presents some difficulties in transliteration. The word we have transliterated as *Gelanggayu* is spelled ڬلڠڬايو . A very similar toponym, Gelang Gui, occurs in the *Sejarah Melayu* or *Malay Annals*, where it is used to denote the place conquered by Raja Shulan, later supplanted by the name Palembang when the Sri Tri Buano dynasty replaced the Shulan dynasty as ruler in Palembang (C.C. Brown 1970). Wolters (1970:95-107) has considered the significance of Gelang Gui and suggests it "must be discarded as a genuine place-name and, instead, be studied as a genealogist's symbol" (Wolters 1970:105). Interestingly, some later versions of the *Sejarah Melayu* state that the name derives from the Thai language (Wolters 1970:97,223, note 73).

16. Gangga Nagara closely resembles the toponym *Gangga Shah Nagara*, which appears in the *Sejarah Melayu* as the first city

conquered by Raja Shulan, the second being *Gelang Gui*.
The *Sejarah Melayu* specifies *Gangga Shah Nagara's* location
as "at Dinding on the other side of the Perak River." See
C.C. Brown (1970:7); see also Wolters (1970:83-84).

17. *Percha, Perca*, or *Percah* are terms which occur in a number
of indigenous works referring to a part or all of Sumatra.
Examples include the *Tuhfat al-Nafis* and the *Hikayat Raja-
Raja Pasai*. A number of toponyms used for part or all of
Sumatra have derived from its products: *Suvarnabhumi*,
Sanskrit for "Land of Gold," *Pulau Lada*, "Pepper Island,"
etc. Perca means india rubber, or caoutchouc, sometimes
also called gutta percha, derived from the sap of several
trees of the sapodilla family (gutta = *getah*, "sap.")
According to Hill (1970:206): "*Pulau Percha*. The origin of
this old name for the southern part of the island of Sumatra
is obscure. To the writer of HRP [Hikayat Raja-Raja Pasai]
it seems to have meant a region bordering the central
highlands in the hinterland of Jambi."

18. The Jukun are a distinct aboriginal ethnic group closer than
the Sakai (see note 8, above) to the coastal Malays in
physique, language, and in their use of agricultural
techniques.

19. *Sikkhari* is a word of Sanskrit origin meaning "mountain" and
is a close toponym to the Thai word Songkhla, the Thai
name for Singgora. Wyatt suggests that both Singgora and
Songkhla may be bastardizations of Sikkhari (personal
communication).

20. *Almarhum*, a word of Arabic origin meaning "the late," is
normally used as a titular prefix added to the personal name
of an individual deserving honor.

21. The Cham, an Austronesian-speaking group, occupied much
of what is now southern Vietnam. They established a
powerful kingdom which endured until overthrown by the
Vietnamese in 1471. There are numerous archaeological
sites, including inscriptions, which mark the former Cham
territories. See Coedes (1968:42-45, 47-48, 56-57, 70-72,
103-4, 122-25, and footnotes).

22. In the *Sejarah Melayu*, Nilatakam (Nila Utama in the current text) was the youngest of three youths who miraculously appeared on Bukit Seguntang, near Palembang. He became raja of Palembang and was given the title *Sang Utama* before being given the new appellation of Sri Tri Buano and voyaging to the islands of Bantam and Tumasik (Singapore). See C.C. Brown (1970:14-21); see also Wolters (1970:77ff) for discussion of the historicity of this personage.

23. Archaeological evidence relating to Srivijaya has been found in several places in south Sumatra, principally in and near modern Palembang. There is no evidence for Srivijaya's existence earlier than the seventh century A.D.; see Miksic (1980).

24. In the *Sejarah Melayu*, a ruler of Nagapatam (a south Indian city) named Raja Shulan conquered many cities in Southeast Asia, including Gangga Shah Nagara and Gelang Gui, whose ruler was Raja Chulin. Raja Shulan's grandson was named Raja Chulan (C.C. Brown 1970:7-9).

25. The name Sailendra has been much discussed by Southeast Asian historians. The name, found in ancient histories of several regions, including Java and Sumatera, contains the significance of "King of the Mountain." However, it is notable that the author makes no mention of the symbolic connections between kingship and mountains, as residences of the gods/ancestors, fertility, Hindu beliefs concerning Siva, and so forth, which are more likely explanations for the use of this term than the idea of mountains as a mere metaphor for power. See Coedes (1966:88-93).

26. A number of temples and other remains in southern Thailand are believed to indicate that Srivijaya once occupied a position of hegemony over the region. Archaeological sites yielding such evidence have included Chaiya and Satingphra. See Diskul (1980); Krairiksh (1980); Lamb (1961); O'Connor (1972); Stargardt (1972).

27. Here the term negeri apparently refers to the constituent states of present-day Malaysia. See note 10, above.

28. See Wolters (1970) on the early rulers of Melaka (Malacca) and the introduction of Islam.

29. *Samsam* is the Malay term used in reference to ethnic Siamese muslims who speak the Thai language and reside in scattered communities in Kedah and Kelantan near the border separating Thailand and Malaysia.

Chapter 2

30. *Maligai* (*Mahligai*, *mahaligai*) is a word of Tamil origin found as a toponym in several places in peninsular Malaysia. It means "pavilion," and carries the connotation of a site connected to a royal court.
31. *Wangsa* or *wamsa* is a common suffix for Sanskritic royal names and designates an extended family or kin group.
32. *Bapak*, frequently shortened as *Pak*, is a respectful term used in addressing men. Bapak (literally "father") is most frequently used for individuals of high status or of greater age than the speaker. Pak is a less formal form of address.
33. Spelled in this case فطابي rather than the form otherwise used throughout this manuscript " فتاني ."
34. When a raja or sultan of Patani died, the author uses the term *mangkat*, which in Malay is normally reserved for use in reference to royalty. Later in the text when the deaths of various Siamese rulers are noted, the author uses the simpler *mati* (literally "to die"), a term used for commoners and all other living things.
35. A *dukun* is a traditional Malay herbal healer. See Gimlette (1975).
36. *Tuan* is a respectful form of address similar to "Sir."
37. Mention of "the Hindu religion" and Buddhist idols and places of worship in the final two sentences of this paragraph reflects the intermingling of Brahmanism and Mahayana Buddhism at that time in Patani, as noted by the author in chapter 1.
38. It is more commonly held that the Portuguese combined both missionary zeal and commercial interests in their eastward expansion. See, for example, Hall (1970:239).

103

39. See Cogan's translation (1969) of *The Voyages and Adventures of Fernand Mendez Pinto*.

40. *Raja Muda* (Literally "young raja") often is translated as "heir apparent." However, as there are numerous instances in Malay history, including that of Patani, where the raja muda is passed over in succession decisions, we have chosen to leave this title untranslated. For a discussion of the status and power of the Malay raja muda see Gullick (1965:61-62).

41. In Malay, the word *amok* (from which derived the English phrase "run amuck") denotes a specific type of behavior, in which an aggrieved person indiscriminately lashes out at all human beings near him without regard for one's own danger; such behavior is frequently a response to a slight upon one's dignity.

42. It is unclear why this name, Raja Patik Siam, was considered to bring luck in this circumstance. *Patik* means "humble servant," and is used as a personal pronoun when addressing royal personages. The literal translation of this title would be "the raja who is the humble servant of Siam."

43. *Okya Decho* is a formal title referring to a military commander, not a personal name. See Teeuw and Wyatt (1970:251).

44. According to Teeuw and Wyatt (1970:9, footnote 41), in the *Royal Chronicles of Ayudhya* a Thai ruler named Phraya Nareswan returned from captivity in Burma in 1571 and began to rebuild his country. He does not appear in the *Hikayat Patani*, however, suggesting that the author did not rely exclusively on this latter source for materials on Patani's history during this period (see Translators' Introduction).

45. Three paragraphs earlier the author stated The Globe arrived at Patani on 23 June.

46. This parenthetical comment is that of the author.

47. This probably refers to a marine festival with boat races. Similar festivals are held in Malaysia today, including the *Main Pantai* or beach festival in Tregganu, which has traditionally included boat races and cultural events such as the *wayang kulit* (shadow play) and the *Mak Yong* (a dance comedy-drama). Often included in these festivities are

propitiatory ceremonies of pre-Islamic origins. Orthodox Muslims frown on such ceremonies, and the Main Pantai today has become simply a social festival.

48. Wyatt (1967:22-23, footnote 21) notes that Professor Wang Gungwu called his attention to a study by Hsu Yun-ts'jao, *Pei-ta-nien shih* (History of Patani), published in Singapore, 1946. According to Hsu, Lim Toh Khiam (Lim Tao-ch'ien) was a famous coastal pirate of the late Ming dynasty who was active off the coasts of Fukien and Kwangtung circa 1566-1573. Professor Hsu suggests that it was after 1578 that Lim Toh Khiam went to settle in Patani. According to the present account, construction of the cannon proceeded circa 1620-1630.

49. This is a key function of a shahbandar (harbor master), but this title was not used by the author in reference to Lim Tho Khiam. As but a few pages later the author refers to a shahbandar in connection with the smuggling of brass needed to make cannon without mentioning Lim, it is probable that Lim's position was something other than shahbandar.

50. The *pokok janggus* is a cashew tree (*Anacardium occidentale*) which grows wild along the coast of Patani. The meaning of *ketirih* is unclear, though there is a climber known as *ketirah* (*Leca indica*). Perhaps the vines were useful in the suicide.

51. This is the author's first explicit reference to a Chinese community within Patani, which apparently was well established by this time.

52. *Toh Pe Kong* in the Hokkien dialect means "temple." The word *mek* in the Kelantan dialect of Malay (closely related to that of Patani) means "young woman."

53. This merchant is referred to as Sheikh Khamu in Wyatt (1967). The same source names the servant as Abdul Mumin.

54. A possible explanation for this name, "Graves of the Long Gentlemen" was suggested to Wyatt (1967) by Professor William Roff. Proper Muslim burial calls for a knees-up, reclining-on-the-side position. Rigor mortis would have prevented this position at the time of their burial, and in

Wyatt's text is was specified that they were buried in an extended position.

55. One *depa* is approximately six feet, or the distance between both hands, when stretched to the side (the fathom in English usage). One *hasta* is equivalent to one cubit, the distance from the elbow to the finger tips. One *jenkal* (*jengkal*) equals the span between thumb and extended forefinger.

56. In Wyatt's text (1967:31), this force was said to consist of 10,000 men who came by land. Their failure was said to be caused by the lack of adequate provisions.

57. The author here used the term *orang Siam* which we have translated as Siamese.

58. Gimlette (1975:65) notes that in Kelantan the *cemara babi* is made of a collection of stiff, dark fibers, each about a foot in length. The cemara babi is said to be "a valuable protecting charm against the charge of a wild boar" (ibid). It is also a protective charm against weapons and is noted as being useful to burglars "because it keeps people in a sound sleep" (ibid). There is no mention made of the cemara babi as a love charm.

59. A *kati* is a measure of weight equal to 1.33 pounds.

60. The author previously stated that the Yang di Pertuan Muda Johor and his people had come from Trengganu, not Johor. However, the author quotes Hamilton in noting that the sultan of Johor had sent one of his trusted ministers to govern in Trengganu, suggesting that the Yang di Pertuan Muda Johor may indeed have returned to Johor rather than Trengganu.

Chapter 3

61. It may be recalled that beginning with Raja Hijau the raja of Siam addressed the female rajas of Patani by a term which was modified by the Malays of Patani as "*Raja Nong Chayang*" (chapter 2). The similarities between Chayang and *Chayam* are intriguing. In jawi orthography the final

consonantal forms of "nga" ($\overset{\cdot\cdot}{\mathcal{E}}$) and "mim" ($\mathcal{C}$) are sufficiently close to suggest a possible printing error. Several such errors were found by the translators in the manuscript.

62. *Kalahom* is the name for both the minister and the Ministry of Military Administration in Thailand. At the end of the seventeenth century this official became responsible for relations between Siam and the provinces and tributary states of the Malay-inhabited region of the peninsula (Teeuw and Wyatt 1970:231).

63. The golden object in the form of a flowering tree and known as *bunga emas* was also sent by Kedah and other Malay states to Bangkok as recognition of Siamese suzerainty. A photograph of a five-tiered Kedah bunga emas is found on the cover of *Kedah Dari Segi Sejarah*, Vol. 4, No. 2 (April 1970).

64. A *tahil* equals 1.33 ounces or 1/16th of a kati (see note 59).

65. Teeuw and Wyatt (1970) name this individual as Raja Bendang Badan (reigned 1716-1720).

66. *Pangkalan* may be translated as "port" (*Pangkalan Besar* = "big port").

67. *Luang* is a Thai term for an official equivalent in rank to "Governor."

68. *Laksamana* is a Malay term for "admiral" or high maritime official. *Dajang* is a toponym; see Wyatt (1975, map 2).

69. *Nik* is a title indicating a degree of genealogical closeness to a ruling line. If the male offspring of a raja marries a non-raja, the children of that union continue to bear the title raja. If, however, a female offspring of a raja marries a non-raja, the children receive the title Nik. The title Nik is likewise inherited through the male line in the case of marriage between a father bearing the title and a non-Nik mother; but should a Nik female marry a non-Nik male, ensuing offspring do not inherit the title.

70. Wyatt has translated a manuscript according to which *Phraya Phraklang* should be *Caophraya Phraklang*, a higher rank, with the distinction between the two corresponding to that between colonel and general, respectively. The source is Phraya Wichiarkhiri (Chom na Songkhla), "Phongsawadan

muang Pattani" (*History of Patani*), in *Prachum phongsawadan* (Collected Chronicles), part 3. The Chronicles were first published in Bangkok in 1914 (in Thai), and reprinted in 1928 and 1964.

71. *Panglima* is a Malay term for a high military commander.

72. Removal of conquered populations to the lands of the victor was a very common act in traditional Southeast Asia. See, for example Reid (1980:243-44).

73. See Wyatt (1974) for a discussion of nineteenth-century Kelantan. The appellation "Red Mouth" doubtlessly refers to this Sultan's penchant for chewing areca, or betel nut.

74. *Lebai* is an honorific used for particularly pious Muslim men.

75. *Tok Ki* literally means "grandfather." Its use here suggests that the man was well beloved by his people.

76. *Bongsu* literally means "last-born" or "youngest," suggesting that this list, with the two daughters at the end, is not in chronological order by birth.

77. *Phraya Si Buriratthaphinit* in Wyatt's unpublished translation (see note 70 above) is *Phra Buriratthaphinit*. This signifies a lower rank than that listed by the author. If phraya is comparable to colonel, phra would be captain. The various Siamese titles and their order of presentation follow precisely that found in Wyatt's translation, indicating that the author had access to the same source.

78. Literally "The Late who died in Kelantan."

79. It appears from the names on the following list that there were two sons and five daughters.

80. This name is somewhat confusing as the word mek refers to a young woman (see note 52 above). Ismail is certainly the name of a man, and Haji is the honorific title for a man who has performed the pilgrimage to Mecca (as opposed to Hajah, the title given to a female pilgrim).

81. The author proceeds to name seven offspring.

82. Compare with the preceding chapter, where the author states that Tungku Abdul Kadir Kamaralludin left for Kelantan soon after his release in 1905.
83. The author proceeds to list five principles.
84. It appears from this that public education was available to the Malay population by the end of the 1930s and was no longer restricted, as the author previously had stated at the beginning of chapter 4, to the children of Siamese officials.
85. At the beginning of this paragraph the letter was said to have been written on 14 January, not 14 February.
86. The Singapore *Straits Times* of 1 December 1948 does not contain an article of Barbara Wittingham-Jones. A search through microfilms of that paper several weeks in either direction failed to turn up this article. However, Wittingham-Jones did write an article in the April 1948 edition of *Eastern World* consistent with the statements the author ascribes to her.
87. *Tikal* = *baht*, the Thai currency.
88. The Islamic Council includes representatives from local mosques who represent Malay Muslim interests to the government and establish local religious policies.
89. This suggests the aerial bombing took place the day before the battle on 28 April noted in the previous paragraph.
90. A *kamnan* is a village headman appointed by the government.
91. See Wittingham-Jones (1948).
92. The chronology of events is somewhat confused. The author's wording suggests the protest letter of February 1948 was received before the 1947 coup. His probable meaning is that this protest was not considered because Phibunsongkhram had returned to power.

REFERENCES

Briggs, L.P. 1951. *The Ancient Khmer empire*. Transactions of the American Philosophical Society. Vol. 41, No. 1: 1-295.

Brown, C.C. (trans.). 1970. *Sejarah Melayu: the Malay Annals*. Kuala Lumpur: Oxford University Press.

Brown, D.E. 1970). *Brunei: the structure and history of a Bornean Malay Sultanate*. Brunei: Brunei Museum Journal Monograph. Vol. 2, No. 2.

Cameron, W. 1883. "On the Patani." *Journal of the Malaysian Branch, Royal Asiatic Society*. Vol. 11: 123-42.

Chew Hock Tong. 1974. "Traditional chiefs in Malaya and Acheh - a reappraisal." *Jernal Antropologi dan Sosiologi*. Vol. 13: 129-37.

Coedes, G. 1968. *The Indianized States of Southeast Asia*. Honolulu: University of Hawaii Press.

Cogan, H. (trans.). 1969. *The Voyages and Adventures of Fernand Mendez Pinto*. London: Dawsons.

Diskul, M.C.S. 1980. Srivijaya art in Thailand. In M.C.S. Diskul (ed.), *The art of Srivijaya*. Kuala Lumpur: Oxford University Press, pp. 21-43.

Dobbin, C. 1975. "The exercise of authority in Minangkabau in the late eighteenth century." In A. Reid and L. Castles (eds.), *Pre-colonial state systems in Southeast Asia*. Kuala Lumpur: Malaysian Branch, Royal Asiatic Society, pp. 77-89.

Gimlette, J.D. 1975. *Malay poisons and charm cures*. Kuala Lumpur: Oxford University Press.

Haemindra, Natawan. 1976. "The problem of the Thai-Muslims in the four southern provinces of Thailand." *Journal of Southeast Asian Studies*. Vol. 7, No. 2: 197-22. (First of two parts.)

Haemindra, Natawan. 1977. "The problem of the Thai-Muslims in the four southern provinces of Thailand." *Journal of Southeast Asian Studies.* Vol. 8, No. 1: 85-105. (Second of two parts.)

Hall, D.G.E. 1970. *A History of South-East Asia.* New York: St. Martin's Press.

Hill, A.H. 1960. "Hikayat Raja-Raja Pasai." *Journal of the Malaysian Branch, Royal Asiatic Society.* Vol. 33, No. 2: 1-215.

Koch, M.L. 1977. "Patani and the development of a Thai state." *Journal of the Malaysian Branch, Royal Asiatic Society.* Vol. 50, No. 2: 69-88.

Krairiksh, P. 1980. *Art in Peninsular Thailand Prior to the Fourteenth century A.D.* Bangkok: Fine Arts Department.

Lamb, A. 1961. "Miscellaneous papers on Hindu and Buddhist settlement in northern Malaya and southern Thailand." *Federation Museums Journal.* Vol. 6: 1-90.

Lewis, M.B. 1954. *A Handbook of Malay Script.* London: MacMillan & Co.

Miksic, J.N. 1980. "Classical Archaeology in Sumatra." *Indonesia.* Vol. 30: 43-64.

Milner, A.C. 1977. "The Malay Raja." Unpublished Ph.D. diss., Cornell University.

O'Connor, S.J. 1972. *Hindu gods of peninsular Siam.* Ascona: Artibus Asiae Publishers.

_____. 1975. "Tambralinga and the Khmer Empire." *Journal of the Siam Society.* Vol. 63, No. 1. 161-76.

Reid, A. 1980. "The Structure of Cities in Southeast Asia, Fifteenth to Seventeenth Centuries." *Journal of Southeast Asian Studies.* Vol. 11, No. 2: 235-50.

Stargardt, J. 1972. "Southern Thai waterways: archaeological evidence on agriculture, shipping and trade in the Srivijayan period." *Man.* Vol. 8, No. 1: 5-29.

Teeuw, A. and D.K. Wyatt. 1970. *Hikayat Patani: The Story of Patani.* 2 Vols. The Hague: M. Nijhoff.

Wales, H.G.Q. 1974. "Langkasuka and Tambralinga: some archaeological notes." *Journal of the Malaysian Branch, Royal Asiatic Society.* Vol. 47: 15-40.

Wheatley, P. 1961. *The Golden Khersonese*. Kuala Lumpur: Pustaka Ilmu.

Wittingham-Jones, B. 1948. "Pattani appeals to UNO." *Eastern World*. Vol. II, No. 4 (April): 4-5.

Wolters, O.W. 1958. "Tambralinga." *Bulletin of the School of Oriental and African Studies*. Vol. 21: 587-607.

_____. 1967. *Early Indonesian Commerce*. Ithaca, N.Y.: Cornell University Press.

_____. 1970. *The Fall of Srivijaya in Malay History*. Ithaca, N.Y.: Cornell University Press.

Wyatt, D.K. 1967. "A Thai Version of Newbold's 'Hikayat Patani.'" *Journal of the Malaysian Branch, Royal Asiatic Society*. Vol. 40, No. 2: 16-37.

_____. 1974. "Nineteenth Century Kelantan: a Thai view." In William Roff (ed.), *Kelantan: Religion, Society, and Politics in a Malay State*. Kuala Lumpur: Oxford University Press.

_____. (trans.). 1975. *The Crystal Sands: The Chronicle of Nagara Sri Dhammaraja*. Ithaca, N.Y.: Cornell University Southeast Asia Program, Data Paper No. 98.

_____. (trans.). Unpublished. "Phongsawadan Muang Pattani (History of Pattani);" by Phraya Wichiankhiri (Chom na Songkhla), in Prachum Phongsawadan (Collected Chronicles), Part 3. First published in 1914, and reprinted in 1928 and 1964.

MONOGRAPHS IN INTERNATIONAL STUDIES

ISBN Prefix 0-89680-

Africa Series

25. Kircherr, Eugene C. ABBYSSINIA TO ZIMBABWE: A Guide to the Political Units of Africa in the Period 1947-1978. 1979. 3rd ed. 80pp.
100-4 $ 8.00*

27. Fadiman, Jeffrey A. MOUNTAIN WARRIORS: The Pre-Colonial Meru of Mt. Kenya. 1976. 82pp.
060-1 $ 4.75*

36. Fadiman, Jeffrey A. THE MOMENT OF CONQUEST: Meru, Kenya, 1907. 1979. 70pp.
081-4 $ 5.50*

37. Wright, Donald R. ORAL TRADITIONS FROM THE GAMBIA: Volume I, Mandinka Griots. 1979. 176pp.
083-0 $12.00*

38. Wright, Donald R. ORAL TRADITIONS FROM THE GAMBIA: Volume II, Family Elders. 1980. 200pp.
084-9 $15.00*

39. Reining, Priscilla. CHALLENGING DESERTIFICATION IN WEST AFRICA: Insights from Landsat into Carrying Capacity, Cultivation and Settlement Site Identification in Upper Volta and Niger. 1979. 180pp., illus.
102-0 $12.00*

41. Lindfors, Bernth. MAZUNGUMZO: Interviews with East African Writers, Publishers, Editors, and Scholars. 1981. 179pp.
108-X $13.00*

42. Spear, Thomas J. TRADITIONS OF ORIGIN AND THEIR INTERPRETATION: The Mijikenda of Kenya. 1982. xii, 163pp.
109-8 $13.50*

43. Harik, Elsa M. and Donald G. Schilling. THE POLITICS OF EDUCATION IN COLONIAL ALGERIA AND KENYA. 1984. 102pp.
117-9 $11.50*

44. Smith, Daniel R. THE INFLUENCE OF THE FABIAN COLONIAL BUREAU ON THE INDEPENDENCE MOVEMENT IN TANGANYIKA. 1985. x, 98pp.
125-X $ 9.00*

45. Keto, C. Tsehloane. AMERICAN-SOUTH AFRICAN RELATIONS 1784-1980: Review and Select Bibliography. 1985. 159pp.
128-4 $11.00*

46. Burness, Don, and Mary-Lou Burness, ed. WANASEMA: Conversations with African Writers. 1985. 95pp.
129-2 $ 9.00*

47. Switzer, Les. MEDIA AND DEPENDENCY IN SOUTH AFRICA: A Case Study of the Press and the Ciskei "Homeland". 1985. 80pp.
130-6   9.00*

48. Heggoy, Alf Andrew. THE FRENCH CONQUEST OF ALGIERS, 1830: An Algerian Oral Tradition. 1986. 101pp.
131-4 $ 9.00*

49. Hart, Ursula Kingsmill. TWO LADIES OF COLONIAL ALGERIA: The Lives and Times of Aurelie Picard and Isabelle Eberhardt. 1987. 156pp.
143-8 $9.00*

50. Voeltz, Richard A. GERMAN COLONIALISM AND THE SOUTH WEST AFRICA COMPANY, 1894-1914. 1988. 143pp.
146-2 $10.00*

51. Clayton, Anthony, and David Killingray. KHAKI AND BLUE: Military and Police in British Colonial Africa. 1989. 235pp.
147-0 $16.00*

52. Northrup, David. BEYOND THE BEND IN THE RIVER: African Labor in Eastern Zaire, 1865-1940. 1988. 195pp.
151-9 $12.00*

53. Makinde, M. Akin. AFRICAN PHILOSOPHY, CULTURE, AND TRADITIONAL MEDICINE. 1988. 175pp.
152-7 $11.00*

55. Burness, Don. A HORSE OF WHITE CLOUDS. 1989. 193pp.
158-6 $10.00*

Latin America Series

1. Frei, Eduardo M. THE MANDATE OF HISTORY AND CHILE'S FUTURE. Tr. by Miguel d'Escoto. Intro. by Thomas Walker. 1977. 79pp.
066-0 $ 8.00*

4. Martz, Mary Jeanne Reid. THE CENTRAL AMERICAN SOCCER WAR: Historical Patterns and Internal Dynamics of OAS Settlement Procedures. 1979. 118pp.
077-6 $ 8.00*

5. Wiarda, Howard J. CRITICAL ELECTIONS AND CRITICAL COUPS: State, Society, and the Military in the Processes of Latin American Development. 1979. 83pp.
082-2 $ 7.00*

6. Dietz, Henry A., and Richard Moore. POLITICAL PARTICIPATION IN A NON-ELECTORAL SETTING: The Urban Poor in Lima, Peru. 1979. viii, 102pp.
085-7 $ 9.00*

7. Hopgood, James F. SETTLERS OF BAJAVISTA: Social and Economic Adaptation in a Mexican Squatter Settlement. 1979. xii, 145pp.
101-2 $11.00*

8. Clayton, Lawrence A. CAULKERS AND CARPENTERS IN A NEW WORLD: The Shipyards of Colonial Guayaquil. 1980. 189pp., illus.
103-9 $15.00*

9. Tata, Robert J. STRUCTURAL CHANGES IN PUERTO RICO'S ECONOMY: 1947-1976. 1981. xiv, 104pp.
107-1 $11.75*

10. McCreery, David. DEVELOPMENT AND THE STATE IN REFORMA GUATEMALA, 1871-1885. 1983. viii, 120pp.
113-6 $ 8.50*

11. O'Shaughnessy, Laura N., and Louis H. Serra. CHURCH AND REVOLUTION IN NICARAGUA. 1986. 118pp.
126-8 $11.00*

12. Wallace, Brian. OWNERSHIP AND DEVELOPMENT: A Comparison of Domestic and Foreign Investment in Columbian Manufacturing. 1987. 186pp.
145-4 $12.00*

13. Henderson, James D. CONSERVATIVE THOUGHT IN LATIN AMERICA: The Ideas of Laureano Gomez. 1988. 150pp.
148-9 $11.00*

14. Summ, G. Harvey, and Tom Kelly. THE GOOD NEIGHBORS: America, Panama, and the 1977 Canal Treaties. 1988. 135pp.
149-7 $11.00*

Southeast Asia Series

31. Nash, Manning. PEASANT CITIZENS: Politics, Religion, and Modernization in Kelantan, Malaysia. 1974. 181pp.
018-0 $12.00*

38. Bailey, Conner. BROKER, MEDIATOR, PATRON, AND KINSMAN: An Historical Analysis of Key Leadership Roles in a Rural Malaysian District. 1976. 79pp.
024-5 $7.00*

40. Van der Veur, Paul W. FREEMASONRY IN INDONESIA FROM RADERMACHER TO SOEKANTO, 1762-1961. 1976. 37pp.
026-1 $4.00*

43. Marlay, Ross. POLLUTION AND POLITICS IN THE PHILIPPINES. 1977. 121pp.
029-6 $7.00*

44. Collier, William L., et al. INCOME, EMPLOYMENT AND FOOD SYSTEMS IN JAVANESE COASTAL VILLAGES. 1977. 160pp.
031-8 $10.00*

45. Chew, Sock Foon and MacDougall, John A. FOREVER PLURAL: The Perception and Practice of Inter-Communal Marriage in Singapore. 1977. 61pp.
030-X $6.00*

47. Wessing, Robert. COSMOLOGY AND SOCIAL BEHAVIOR IN A WEST JAVANESE SETTLEMENT. 1978. 200pp.
072-5 $12.00*

48. Willer, Thomas F., ed. SOUTHEAST ASIAN REFERENCES IN THE BRITISH PARLIAMENTARY PAPERS, 1801-1972/73: An Index. 1978. 110pp.
033-4 $ 8.50*

49. Durrenberger, E. Paul. AGRICULTURAL PRODUCTION AND HOUSEHOLD BUDGETS IN A SHAN PEASANT VILLAGE IN NORTHWESTERN THAILAND: A Quantitative Description. 1978. 142pp.
071-7 $9.50*

50. Echauz, Robustiano. SKETCHES OF THE ISLAND OF NEGROS. 1978. 174pp.
070-9 $10.00*

51. Krannich, Ronald L. MAYORS AND MANAGERS IN THAILAND: The   Struggle   for   Political   Life   in Administrative Settings. 1978. 139pp.
073-3 $ 9.00*

54. Ayal, Eliezar B., ed.   THE STUDY OF THAILAND: Analyses of Knowledge, Approaches, and Prospects in Anthropology, Art History, Economics, History and Political Science. 1979. 257pp.
079-2 $13.50*

56A. Duiker, William J. VIETNAM SINCE THE FALL OF SAIGON. Updated edition. 1989. 383pp.
162-4 $14.00*

57. Siregar, Susan Rodgers.   ADAT, ISLAM, AND CHRISTIANITY IN A BATAK HOMELAND.   1981. 108pp.
110-1 $10.00*

58. Van Esterik, Penny. COGNITION AND DESIGN PRODUCTION IN BAN CHIANG POTTERY. 1981. 90pp. 078-4 $12.00*

59. Foster, Brian L. COMMERCE AND ETHNIC DIFFERENCES: The Case of the Mons in Thailand. 1982. x, 93pp. 112-8 $10.00*

60. Frederick, William H., and John H. McGlynn. REFLECTIONS ON REBELLION: Stories from the Indonesian Upheavals of 1948 and 1965. 1983. vi, 168pp. 111-X $ 9.00*

61. Cady, John F. CONTACTS WITH BURMA, 1935-1949: A Personal Account. 1983. x, 117pp. 114-4 $ 9.00*

62. Kipp, Rita Smith, and Richard D. Kipp, eds. BEYOND SAMOSIR: Recent Studies of the Batak Peoples of Sumatra. 1983. viii, 155pp. 115-2 $ 9.00*

63. Carstens, Sharon, ed. CULTURAL IDENTITY IN NORTHERN PENINSULAR MALAYSIA. 1986. 91pp. 116-0 $ 9.00*

64. Dardjowidjojo, Soenjono. VOCABULARY BUILDING IN INDONESIAN: An Advanced Reader. 1984. xviii, 256pp. 118-7 $26.00*

65. Errington, J. Joseph. LANGUAGE AND SOCIAL CHANGE IN JAVA: Linguistic Reflexes of Modernization in a Traditional Royal Polity. 1985. xiv, 198pp. 120-9 $12.00*

66. Binh, Tran Tu. THE RED EARTH: A Vietnamese Memoir of Life on a Colonial Rubber Plantation. Tr. by John Spragens. Ed. by David Marr. 1985. xii, 98pp. 119-5 $ 9.00*

68. Syukri, Ibrahim. HISTORY OF THE MALAY KINGDOM OF PATANI. Tr. by Conner Bailey and John N. Miksic. 1985. xix, 113pp.
123-3 $12.50*

69. Keeler, Ward. JAVANESE: A Cultural Approach. 1984. xxxvi, 523pp.
121-7 $18.00*

70. Wilson, Constance M., and Lucien M. Hanks. BURMA-THAILAND FRONTIER OVER SIXTEEN DECADES: Three Descriptive Documents. 1985. x, 128pp.
124-1 $10.50*

71. Thomas, Lynn L., and Franz von Benda-Beckmann, eds. CHANGE AND CONTINUITY IN MINANGKABAU: Local, Regional, and Historical Perspectives on West Sumatra. 1986. 363pp.
127-6 $14.00*

72. Reid, Anthony, and Oki Akira, eds. THE JAPANESE EXPERIENCE IN INDONESIA: Selected Memoirs of 1942-1945. 1986. 411pp., 20 illus.
132-2 $18.00*

73. Smirenskaia, Zhanna D. PEASANTS IN ASIA: Social Consciousness and Social Struggle. Tr. by Michael J. Buckley. 1987. 248pp.
134-9 $12.50

74. McArthur, M.S.H. REPORT ON BRUNEI IN 1904. Ed. by A.V.M. Horton. 1987. 304pp.
135-7 $13.50

75. Lockard, Craig Alan. FROM KAMPUNG TO CITY. A Social History of Kuching Malaysia 1820-1970. 1987. 311pp.
136-5 $14.00*

76. McGinn, Richard. STUDIES IN AUSTRONESIAN LINGUISTICS. 1988. 492pp.
137-3 $18.50*

77. Muego, Benjamin N. SPECTATOR SOCIETY: The Philippines Under Martial Rule. 1988. 232pp.
138-1 $12.50*

78. Chew, Sock Foon. ETHNICITY AND NATIONALITY IN SINGAPORE. 1987. 229pp.
139-X $12.50*

79. Walton, Susan Pratt. MODE IN JAVANESE MUSIC. 1987. 279pp.
144-6 $12.00*

80. Nguyen Anh Tuan. SOUTH VIETNAM TRIAL AND EXPERIENCE: A Challenge for Development. 1987. 482pp.
141-1 $15.00*

81. Van der Veur, Paul W., ed. TOWARD A GLORIOUS INDONESIA: Reminiscences and Observations of Dr. Soetomo. 1987. 367pp.
142-X $13.50*

82. Spores, John C. RUNNING AMOK: An Historical Inquiry. 1988. 190pp.
140-3 $13.00*

83. Tan Malaka. FROM JAIL TO JAIL. Tr. and ed. by Helen Jarvis. 1990. 3 vols. 1200pp.
150-0 $45.00*

84. Devas, Nick. FINANCING LOCAL GOVERNMENT IN INDONESIA. 1989. 344pp.
153-5 $14.00*

85. Suryadinata, Leo. MILITARY ASCENDANCY AND POLITICAL CULTURE: A Study of Indonesia's Golkar. 1989. 222pp.
179-9 $11.50*

86. Williams, Michael. COMMUNISM, RELIGION, AND REVOLT IN BANTEN. 1990. 356pp.
155-1 $14.00*

ORDERING INFORMATION

Orders for titles in the Monographs in International Studies series should be placed through the Ohio University Press/Scott Quadrangle/Athens, Ohio 45701-2979. Individuals must remit pre-payment via check, VISA, MasterCard, CHOICE, or American Express. Individuals ordering from the United Kingdom, Continental Europe, Middle East, and Africa should order through Academic and University Publishers Group, 1 Gower Street, London WC1E 6HA, England. Other individuals ordering from outside of the U.S., please remit in U.S. funds by either International Money Order or check drawn on a U.S. bank. Postage and handling is $2.00 for the first book and $.50 for each additional book. Prices and availability are subject to change without notice.

CPSIA information can be obtained
at www.ICGtesting.com
Printed in the USA
LVHW090818151020
668831LV00003B/6